Protecting Your Assets

ALSO BY ANDREW D. WESTHEM

Winning the Wealth Game (with Donald Jay Korn)

ALSO BY DONALD JAY KORN

Audit-Proof Tax Shelters
Your Money or Your Life
High-Powered Investing (with Gary Goldberg)
Winning the Wealth Game (with Andrew D. Westhem)

Protecting Your Assets

How to Safeguard and Maintain Your Personal Wealth

Andrew D. Westhem
and
Donald Jay Korn

A Citadel Press Book
Published by Carol Publishing Group

A Citadel Press Book
Published by Carol Publishing Group
Citadel Press is a registered trademark of Carol Communications, Inc.
Editorial Offices: 600 Madison Avenue, New York, N.Y. 10022
Sales and Distribution Offices: 120 Enterprise Avenue, Secaucus, N.J. 07094
In Canada: Canadian Manda Group, One Atlantic Avenue, Suite 105,
    Toronto, Ontario M6K 3E7
Queries regarding rights and permissions should be addressed to
Carol Publishing Group, 600 Madison Avenue, New York, N.Y. 10022

Carol Publishing Group books are available at special discounts for bulk purchases, sales promotions, fund-raising, or educational purposes. Special editions can be created to specifications. For details, contact Special Sales Department, Carol Publishing Group, 120 Enterprise Avenue, Secaucus, N.J. 07094

Manufactured in the United States of America
10 9 8 7 6 5 4 3 2 1

Westhem, Andrew D., 1933-
    Protecting your assets : how to safeguard and maintain your personal wealth / Andrew D. Westhem and Donald Jay Korn.
        p.   cm.
    "A Citadel Press book."
    ISBN 0-8065-1760-3 (pbk.)
    1. Finance, Personal.   2. Financial security.   I. Korn, Donald Jay.   II. Title.
HG179.W475 1996
332.024--dc20   96-348
                                                                            CIP

To all the honest, reliable,
service-oriented financial professionals
who are dedicated to helping
their clients protect hard-won assets

Contents

Acknowledgments

Since helping people protect assets, property, and themselves comes first, I would like to thank my partners and associates at Wealth Transfer Planning, Inc., Earl Eastman, Rolf Benirschke, Susan Joyce, William Storum, and Cory Grant.

Western Capital Financial's hardworking specialists who have spent the last ten years helping their clients, on a national basis, protect themselves against income taxes.

Thank you to Wealth Transfer Planning, Inc.'s nationally affiliated attorneys who have played such an important role in assisting us in the asset protection portion of this book. They are: Steven Sciarretta, William George, Stephen Margolin, Larry Bell, and Robin Klomparins.

Our newsletter editor friends who are greatly responsible for the general idea of the book. These editors are Mark Skousen, Richard Band, Peter Dickenson, William Donoghue, and Joseph Bradley.

Those whose seminars have enabled us to bring these ideas to the public: Kim and Charles Githler of Investment Seminars Incorporated and James Blanchard of Blanchard Seminars.

Samantha Hudson, whose public relations expertise opens new avenues to travel.

Bambi Holzer, whose expertise in the qualified retirement plan field has been extremely valuable to us.

Martin M. Shenkman, attorney at law, Teaneck, N.J.

A special thank you to my ever understanding and loving wife,

Emily; to my daughter, Lisa, my son David, and my daughter-in-law, Alicia. To my first grandchild, Ashley, the apple of my eye.

I would like to especially acknowledge my father, David S. Westheim (1890–1976), whose teachings and philosophies on protecting your sales territory and clients were invaluable to me.

Introduction

Keeping What We Have

Not everybody is driven by ambition to become wealthy. For every person who works one hundred hours a week, fifty-two weeks a year, to further a career, there are many who are content to put in their forty hours and devote leisure time to friends and family.

However, there is one thread that binds us all, no matter how we pursue wealth: We want to keep what we have. No one likes the idea of losing capital, whether to a thief or a con artist or an act of nature. What's more, we're all concerned with the well-being of our loved ones, as well as of ourselves.

Today, though, keeping what's yours isn't easy. You can be physically attacked in your house or your car or on the street where you live. A hurricane or an earthquake (for example) can destroy your home. If you stretch for extra yield, in today's puny three-percent environment, you have to take on more risks and expose yourself to unscrupulous predators.

Threats to your wealth can generate more perils. When an earthquake shook southern California in early 1994, Paula W. suffered considerable damage to her house. Moreover, her chimney was left at a perilous angle, leaning over the driveway of her next-door neighbor who was pregnant. Desperate, she hired a contractor to tear down the chimney, paying $1,500. The job, performed by three men, took only twenty minutes. Later, Paula learned that some of her neighbors had paid as little as $100 for similar work. She had been taken as well as shaken.

Some inroads into your wealth can be larger—*much* larger. George K., a Pittsburgh executive, decided to buy shares in a video store company for three cents per share, investing a total of $600. Over the next three years, encouraged by press releases, a broker's reassurances, and phone conversations with the company's president, George and members of his family built up a $100,000 stake. The stock, it turned out, was no blockbuster. Share prices moved up for a while, but then collapsed. After the company filed for bankruptcy in 1991, George and his fellow investors held virtually worthless stock. What's more, after he paid another $5,000 to an arbitration firm, the hearing went against him, adding financial insult to injury.

There seems to be no end to the ways in which promoters can separate investors from their money. In April 1994, one issue of the *Wall Street Journal* contained articles on an eight-state roundup of fraudulent wireless-communications deals, on federal charges against a firm selling movie posters as collectors' items, and on federal action against a company offering "guaranteed" annual returns of 10 percent–14 percent to investors who would make auto loans. In southern California alone, state regulators estimated that thirty phone-scam artists were ripping off investors to the tune (or tone) of $30 million per month.

Of course, "keeping what we have" means more than wealth preservation, in today's increasingly violent world. In 1992 (the latest year for which statistics were available as of this writing), over 1,000 Americans were murdered on the job, 32 percent higher than the rate in the not-exactly-pacific 1980s. In a 1994 survey by the American Management Association (AMA), nearly a quarter of the companies responding said that at least some employees had been murdered or attacked since 1990. Not only are you not safe at home, in your car, or walking on the streets, but you can't let your guard down at work, either.

With all the risks out there, your margin of error is slim. One serious illness can wipe out an uninsured family. One adverse judgment, handed down by an increasingly capricious legal system, can literally take away your life's work.

We all saw how Hurricane Andrew destroyed thousands of homes. There's not much you can do when you're in the path of an awesome storm, but (especially with the help of this book) at least you can make sure beforehand that you have the *right* kind of insurance coverage, with the *right* company, so that your house will be replaced.

The *wrong* kind of insurance company can cause irreparable damage in other areas of your life, also. For example, thousands of investors were victimized when both Executive Life and Mutual Benefit Life (and others) were seized by state regulators. Many people had suffered heavy losses on annuities and guaranteed investment contracts. If you pick a *healthy* insurance company, you won't be vulnerable to such disasters.

Today you need to play defense, whether or not you play offense. That's why we've written this book. We want to show you what you can do—*must do*—to protect yourself against catastrophic losses. Our advice is practical rather than theoretical, with many examples to help you see what kind of action to take in which sort of situation.

In this book, we begin by showing you how to invest profitably, yet safely. From there, we explain how to buy the right kind of insurance for your house and your car. We go on to show how to protect your career, how to keep your guard up while you travel, how to buy health insurance without getting sick from the bills, how to preserve your wealth in retirement, how to avoid disastrous lawsuits, how to keep your assets intact in case of a divorce, and how to pass on what you've earned to your family. Finally, we show you how to protect the most important things you have—yourself and your family. Our aim in this book is to provide guidance for everyone with something to protect—and that means *everyone*.

Part I

Get Rich Slowly

1

No Gains Without Potential Pain

Invest Profitably Without Taking Undue Risk

There was a time when school revolved around the "three R's": reading, 'riting, and 'rithmetic. Although those days are long gone, investing still depends on the "two R's": risk and reward.

Low-risk investments offer low rewards. A Treasury bill issued by the federal government, for example, pays a low interest rate. If T-bills paid high rates, investors would scramble to buy them and the increased demand would drive up the price. As the price went up, the yield would keep dropping until it was in line with the low level of risk.

Conversely, the stock of a start-up biotech company must offer the potential of high returns to lure investors into a risky venture. Once the stock price goes too high, further rewards will seem unlikely and

3

investors will stop buying. Eventually, the price will drop to a level where there's the potential for huge gains.

No matter what anyone tells you, you can't escape the risk–reward matrix. After all, if you seek high returns, you'll have to take *some* risks. The trick is to keep the risks manageable while making investments that truly *have* potentially high returns.

Keep a Stash of Cash

Most investors play it too safe. That is, they keep too much of their money in bank accounts or money-market funds. These vehicles are extremely low-risk because you're not likely to suffer from defaults or trading losses associated with them. Therefore, they offer low returns. In early 1994, for example, six-month certificates of deposits (CDs) paid an average of 2.7 percent, the same as money-market funds. After-tax, you'd likely wind up with less than 2 percent—not enough to keep up with inflation.

Most people should keep a minimal amount in "cash equivalents": bank accounts, money-market funds, or T-bills. Besides low risk, they offer easy access to your cash in case of an emergency. Generally, you should keep one-third to one-fourth of a year's income in cash equivalents, where you can get at your money quickly. The rest you should hold in longer-term investments, where the potential rewards are greater.

Bank Notes

Some people prefer to keep more of their money in cash equivalents. They're so averse to taking any risks that they're willing to accept the low returns. That's fine when it comes to T-bills, which have the full backing of the U.S. government. Also, money-market funds have proven to be super-safe investments over their relatively short history. For safety's sake, use a money fund offered by a well-established brokerage firm or mutual-fund family.

Bank accounts, though, are a different story. From 1987 through the writing of this book, over 1,000 U.S. banks, holding a total of more than $150 billion in assets, failed. What happens when your bank fails? Deposits *of any size* are insured up to only $100,000.

That wasn't enough for Jerold and Judith S., who wired a maturing $99,000 CD to their joint account at Atlantic Financial Savings in

Pittsburgh, bringing their balance to $147,000—most of the money they had managed to save on Jerold's salary as a college professor. Jerold and Judith planned to invest $100,000 in municipal bonds within a week. Before they could act, though, Atlantic failed. They got back their $100,000, but it was still uncertain, as of last report, whether they'd ever get back the other $47,000.

Even if you stick to the $100,000 limit, you can get burned by a bank closing. Judy T., a third-grade teacher in Wilton, Connecticut, kept $145,000 in Resource Savings of Denison, Texas, selected for its high, federally insured rates. She put $100,000 in her own name, and the other $45,000 in joint accounts with her children.

When Resource went under in 1990, federal regulators stepped in, and Judy had to wait five weeks before she could get her money out. She didn't lose any of the principal, but she lost all the earnings on her $100,000 CD (because those earnings were over the limit), plus five weeks' interest on her other CDs. Altogether, she lost more than $2,000.

Be careful with your bank accounts. For example, *never* keep more than $100,000 in the same bank under the same name: You need to spread your money among several accounts (perhaps one in your name and one in the name of your spouse or a "significant other")— even several banks. And try to avoid banks in shaky financial condition. For an evaluation of your bank, call Veribanc (800-442-2657) or Bauer Financial Reports (800-388-6686).

Take an Interest in Bonds

After you have your emergency money in a money-market fund and/ or safe bank, you can start thinking about potentially higher-yield investments. The first step up from cash equivalents is the bond market. The principle is the same—you're lending your money in return for interest. When you invest in bonds, though, you're lending money for longer time periods, perhaps as long as thirty years.

The bond market actually breaks down into two categories: Treasuries, and everything else. Treasury notes (maturing in two to ten years) and bonds (out to thirty years) are do-it-yourself investments. You can buy Treasuries on your own, with little or no fee, from banks or brokers or the Federal Reserve. The only real risk is market risk: If interest rates go up, the value of your bonds will fall. But if you hold your bonds until maturity, this risk disappears. So stick to Treasuries maturing in eight years or less, to get a decent yield with minimal risk.

Other types of bonds pay higher yields, but they're not for most investors. That is, investors shouldn't buy these bonds directly. There is a great deal you need to know about—credit risk, market risk, call risk, reinvestment risk—and relatively little information available about each issue. In the related area of mortgage-backed securities, such as Ginnie Maes and collateralized mortgage obligations (CMOs), there's even more you need to know, such as the assumed speed of prepayments and the amortization of discounts or premiums.

In general, the only people who should invest in non-Treasury bonds are those with at least $50,000 to spread around ten different issues. Thus, your portfolio can survive a disaster that strikes any one issue. In addition, you should either be financially sophisticated about the bond market, or work with a broker or financial planner who is.

Few investors can meet those criteria. Fortunately, other investors have another path to investing in the bond market: no-load mutual funds. You may give up some potential reward when you turn to funds instead of investing directly in bonds, but you greatly reduce your risk.

Mutual funds can invest in dozens of different issues, so the risks are spread widely. Bonds are selected by full-time investment professionals who know the market. Mutual funds are particularly good vehicles for Ginnie Maes and CMOs because all prepayments are automatically reinvested, sparing you the headache thereof. Generally, you can invest in mutual funds for as little as $2,500 or $3,000.

Best Bond Buys

When you invest in bond mutual funds, you have hundreds to choose among. How can you pick the ones that will protect you from loss even while generating a substantial return?

• *Buy funds that have no sales charge and no redemption fee.* If you do your own research, you might as well buy a no-load. If you rely on a broker for advice, you'll have to pay a commission, reducing the amount you have working for you.

• *Buy the right type of fund.* It doesn't make sense to buy Treasuries through a mutual fund. Corporate bond funds and Ginnie Mae funds are most appropriate for investors in a low tax bracket, or for holding in a tax-sheltered retirement plan. If you're in a high bracket, investing outside of a retirement plan, municipal bond funds may be your best choice.

• *Look carefully at a fund's holdings.* If you buy a fund holding long-term bonds (average maturity of twenty years or more), you're vulnerable to interest-rate swings. Funds with average maturities under ten years are safer.

• *Buy seasoned funds with a good record.* Why buy a new fund when you can buy one that's been around five years or longer and has shown what it can do? Pick a fund based on total return rather than current yield: A high yield doesn't help if the share value of your bond fund goes down.

Perhaps the safest bond fund you can own, yet still earn high yields, is Vanguard Bond Index Fund (800-662-7447), which aims to duplicate the total return of Salomon Brothers Broad Investment-Grade Bond Index. The fund's expenses are extremely low. From its inception at the end of 1986 through 1993, the price stayed between $9 and $10.25 per share; average maturity is about ten years. The fund's total return was over 10 percent a year during this period.

A slightly better performance (over 11 percent per year) was registered by Harbor Bond Fund (800-422-1050). This fund holds a mix of bonds, everthing from Federal National Mortgage Association (Fannie Mae) to Chrysler. Again, the average maturity is around ten years, and share-price volatility has been moderate.

As mentioned, mortgage-backed securities go particularly well in mutual funds because *all* prepayments are reinvested. Managers Intermediate Mortgage Securities (800-835-3879) generated the top return in the 1989–93 period, nearly 14 percent per year, despite keeping maturities to an average of only six years, thus holding down risk. If you're looking for a straight Ginnie Mae fund (Ginnie Maes are extra-safe because they're fully backed by the federal government), Vanguard Fixed-Income GNMA (800-662-7447) has an excellent record, with *no* down years since its founding in 1980.

Among municipal bond funds, both Scudder Medium-Term Tax-Free Fund (800-225-2470) and USAA Tax-Exempt Intermediate-Term Fund (800-382-8722) have splendid records, protecting investors from loss of principal. Average maturities typically range between eight and nine years, so fluctuations in share prices have been modest.

No matter which bond fund you choose, ask for *dividend reinvestment*. Over the years the share value likely will stay fairly constant, yet your balance will grow as the reinvested dividends compound. With a diversified, intermediate-term bond fund, you're not likely to see your investment slip away from you.

Stock Answers

Investing in stocks is similar to investing in bonds. You should buy stocks directly only if you have the patience to do thorough research and the means to hold shares in ten or more companies. To protect your portfolio, those companies should be spread among different sectors of the economy rather than concentrated in one or two industries.

The safest investments are in companies that pay substantial dividends and have done so for many years—those companies consistently generate more cash than they need. Don't invest in the hot tip you've heard about in the locker room unless you already have a portfolio of blue-chips.

One possible strategy is to emphasize companies with a long history of increasing dividends. In early 1994, for example, Bic Corp., North America's largest maker of ballpoint pens and disposable lighters, increased its dividend for the eighth time in nine years; Bic has paid dividends every year since going public in 1971. When you invest in a company like this, you're fairly certain that your ownership stake will retain value and probably grow.

If you don't want to pick stocks yourself, there are mutual funds from which you can choose. There are many types of stock funds, everything from international funds to small-company funds to funds that specialize in one sector of the economy. Although some specialty funds may have excellent results, your principal probably is safest if you buy diversified funds that invest in a cross-section of U.S. stocks. Moreover, you want to look for a solid, long-term track record. The following no-loads fit that description, having posted average total returns of 16–17 percent per year for the ten years that ended in 1993:
- Berger 100 (800-333-1001)
- SteinRoe Special Fund (800-338-2550)
- Twentieth Century Ultra Investors (800-345-2021)

Again, if you *reinvest* dividends, your fund balance likely will grow over the long term, overriding any market losses.

Some discount brokers, such as Charles Schwab, will handle orders for no-load mutual funds. You may be able to buy more than 200 funds without paying transaction costs, and you'll enjoy the convenience of having your no-load funds summarized on a single statement.

Discount brokers may offer to let you buy mutual funds *on margin*—which is to say that you may be able to buy funds with up to 50 percent borrowed money. For most investors, however, buying on margin isn't a good idea. The same goes for buying individual stocks on margin. Investing in stocks is risky enough without investing with money that's not even yours.

Grow Now, Pay Tax Later

There's yet another investment option if you want asset growth and protection: buying deferred annuities. You give money to an insurance company or another financial institution, in one large payment or a series of payments. The earnings can grow, tax-deferred, until you withdraw your funds.

Deferred annuities can be either *fixed* or *variable*. With a *fixed* annuity, your money will earn a bondlike return each year, yet your principal won't shrink if the bond market declines. You have upside, but no downside.

Variable annuities give you a choice of investment vehicles, usually including several mutual funds. You can invest in the stock market if you want, with a shot at superior long-term results. Your account may fall, it's true, but variable annuities pay a death benefit to your beneficiaries that's guaranteed to be no lower than the money you invested.

How can you pick safe annuities? With a *fixed* annuity, start with the financial strength of the insurance company issuing it. The insurer should be rated A+ by A. M. Best, and AA or better by Standard & Poor's, Moody's, or Duff & Phelps. If you invest with a weak insurer, lured by the appeal of high interest rates, you risk the fate of those who bought Baldwin-United annuities: After the company became insolvent in 1983, annuity investors had to wait as long as four years to get any money out of their contracts. To find out how an insurer is rated, ask at your local library for insurance industry reference books.

The other key criterion is the company's history of renewal rates. You don't want an insurer that lured investors with an 11 percent yield several years ago, then gradually reduced renewal rates to 4 percent while continuing to use high come-on rates for new buyers. Ask to see the renewal record, and check on whether old investors are getting approximately the same deal as new ones.

Safe Harbors

As we have to some extent already demonstrated, variable annuities are different from fixed annuities. You don't need to be as concerned about insurance company safety because variable-annuity money goes into separate accounts, not into the insurance company's general account. Thus, if the insurance company runs into trouble, variable-annuity investors will not be lumped with other creditors—their funds will remain separate.

With a variable annuity, the big concern is the quality of the people managing your money. You should be looking for "name brand" mutual-fund managers, such as John Templeton and Martin Zweig and the people who manage funds for Fidelity, Janus, T. Rowe Price, and so on. Then you know you'll enjoy first-rate money management. Some variable annuities, in fact, are so confident of their managers' abilities that they'll guarantee paying a 5 percent or 7 percent annual profit to your beneficiaries if you die while holding a deferred annuity.

What if you're already in an annuity (fixed *or* variable) and become disenchanted? If you simply pull out of the contract, you'll owe surrender charges, income taxes, *and* possible penalties.

For example, Miles and Ann J. of Los Angeles invested $26,000 in a Pacific Standard Life Insurance annuity in 1988. In 1989, the troubled insurer was taken over by the state of California. Miles and Ann asked for their money back, and got a refund—after seven months of correspondence. However, even though their account had grown to nearly $30,000, they got back only $27,000—they lost $2,600 in surrender charges. Plus, they owed taxes and penalties on their $1,000 gain.

Miles and Ann would have been better off if they had acted sooner. They could have contacted an agent specializing in annuities, and switched to a better contract: You can execute a "1035 exchange" from one annuity (or life-insurance policy) to another and owe *no* income tax. You might pay a surrender charge, but that's better than staying with a subpar annuity.

Assuming you find a good contract to begin with, are annuities right for you? They should be considered supplementary retirement plans, to be purchased *after* you have funded your deductible IRA, Keogh, 401(k), etc. If you have excess money to invest, and you can keep your hands off that money until you reach age 59½, then deferred annuities are a tax-advantaged way to enjoy asset growth as well as safety.

SUMMING UP

- The key to investment success is to take measured risks while putting your money into vehicles with real growth potential.
- Don't keep more than a few months' worth of income in cash equivalents, such as bank accounts or money-market funds.
- Stick with financially strong banks and keep your accounts under $100,000, the limit for federal insurance.
- Although Treasury bonds may be bought directly, other types of bonds should be bought through no-load mutual funds (unless you're an extremely sophisticated investor).
- If you're a diligent investor, you can pick your own stocks, emphasizing established, dividend-paying companies.
- Most investors are better off buying stocks through mutual funds.
- Look for funds with solid, long-term records, and *reinvest* your dividends.
- Deferred annuities can provide investment safety *and* tax-advantaged growth.
- Look for a financially strong insurer when you buy a *fixed* annuity, and for first-class mutual-fund managers when you buy a *variable* annuity.
- Annuities should be a supplementary source of retirement funds, most appropriate for those who can do without the money until age 59½ (and thus avoid a tax penalty).

2

Getting Churned Is Getting Burned

How to Keep Your Broker Honest

Back in the late 1980s, Joseph F. was worried. He was a retired construction supervisor in Phoenix who had been treated for cancer. He and his wife had saved their money but were concerned about how long it would last. So when he received a call from a broker, he listened.

The broker, after all, worked for one of the top brokerage firms in the country, one that spends millions of dollars on TV ads touting its investment savvy. He told Joseph to pull all of his money out of insured bank accounts and get "more safety," along with high yields, in a "Triple-A rated" junk-bond fund.

The result? In just over a year, Joseph's $115,000 nest egg was worth less than $40,000.

Unfortunately, Joseph's story is hardly unique. William and Donna B. of California went to the Century City office of another big-name brokerage firm, where they were referred to one of the "star" brokers.

12

This broker even appeared regularly on local TV, giving investment advice. What more could they ask?

A few years later, William and Donna had lost $200,000 in a series of worthless limited partnerships.

Such horror stories could make up a book of their own. There are about 200,000 licensed brokers in the United States, most of whom are law-abiding citizens. Even a small percentage of bad apples, however, means hundreds, even thousands of brokers you need to watch out for, at large firms as well as small ones. One broker, in fact, moved some losing options investments from his personal account to clients' accounts, so his clients would pay for his losses.

Pieces of the Action

Most broker abuses involve the practice of *churning*. Brokers work on commission—every time you buy or sell securities, you pay a sales fee. So some brokers are *not* satisfied by telling you to buy AT&T and hold on until you retire. Instead, they'll tell you that what you have now is *wrong*—no matter *what* it is. You *must* sell, and buy something else!

A few months later, after their "sure thing" is down sharply, you're again told to sell, and to buy something else. This "churning" goes on and on, from one flaky investment to the next, while your portfolio value shrinks and the broker's commission income expands. (Some investors even sign discretionary agreements giving brokers the authority to trade their accounts *without* prior approval—an open invitation to churning.)

What can you do to avoid being victimized? Start by writing down your financial goals. You might, for example, say that preservation of capital is your primary objective, followed by long-term growth. Have your broker sign a copy. Once someone puts his or her name on a document, there's a marked tendency to live up to the stated terms.

Don't sign discretionary trading agreements. Rather, keep your eye on your monthly statements, to see how much trading activity is taking place. If more than 25 percent of your stocks turn over each year, you should find out why your account is so active.

What if you don't have the time or inclination to ride herd on your broker and approve all trades in advance? Most firms now offer "wrap" accounts, even to small investors. Here, you turn over your portfolio's management to a professional, paying a fee of around 3 percent of funds under management. That is, a $100,000 investor would pay around $3,000 per year for all brokerage costs, including commissions. That's a substantial amount, but it's far better than falling victim to a broker who churns your account.

If you do maintain control over your own investing, exercise caution. Don't believe in get-rich-quick schemes—no stock is "guaranteed" to double in a month, or even a year. New offerings and very small stocks are speculative, so don't overload. Build a solid base of proven stocks and investment-grade bonds before allocating a portion of your holdings to more-speculative issues.

Don't Call Us

If you suspect you've been victimized by your broker, how should you proceed? One thing you *shouldn't* do is call the Securities and Exchange Commission (SEC). But that's precisely what Lawrence V., a Glendora, California, building contractor, did. Proceeding on the advice of one SEC staffer, Lawrence wrote up a thirty-page report detailing his $100,000 loss. A month later, he received a two-page *form* letter saying that the SEC couldn't help him.

Your best bet is probably to go through channels at your brokerage firm. Complain to your broker, the branch manager, and the firm's compliance department. If all of that doesn't help, see a lawyer who specializes in securities law. (Your local bar association probably will be able to recommend someone.) Don't delay, because you may miss out on a deadline for bringing an action. Such deadlines vary from state to state, but the general rule is that you must act within a year or so of discovering that you've been defrauded.

You may be able to file a lawsuit, but in many cases you'll then be forced to go through arbitration, under the terms of your brokerage agreement. *Arbitration* is an expedited process during which your case is heard by a panel of experts. Chances are, you'll wind up with a partial recovery in far less time than would be the case if you brought a lawsuit. Arbitration hearings usually last one or two days, with resolution expectable within a year of filing.

Even though it's not required, you're best off retaining a securities lawyer if you go through arbitration. If your dispute involves $30,000 or more, you'll likely be able to find and hire an experienced securities lawyer. Even if you have a smaller claim, you probably can get a consultation with a lawyer for either a token fee or no fee at all.

What you're looking for is an indication that you'll have a good chance of succeeding, should you press your case. For example, if your broker misled you about expected results, you probably are in a strong position to win some restitution. The same holds if the broker sold you unsuitable securities—as would be shares in a start-up gold-mining company, if you're a widow depending on fixed income, for example.

Stake Your Claim

If you decide to proceed on your own, the National Association of Securities Dealers (NASD) offers arbitration. Call 212-858-4400 for an arbitration kit.

Whichever way you go for arbitration, do-it-yourself or with a lawyer, you'll need to file a *statement of claim,* which will become the basis of your case. In this statement, you'll explain what happened, and why you think you should get your money back.

Give as much detail as possible. If you say your account was churned, tell how many trades were executed and in what time period. Attach copies of the brokerage statements to support your allegations.

If you're claiming that the broker made misrepresentations, tell exactly (to the best of your recollection) what he or she said, and when. Attach any correspondence or promotional materials you received that made inflated claims.

Usually, disputes of $10,000 or less will be decided *without* a hearing, but rather based on the paperwork you submit. Disputes concerning between $10,000 and $30,000 will be heard by a single arbitrator. However, for smaller claims you have the right to request a hearing with *three* arbitrators. The stronger your case, the better off you are with a trio, because you risk losing, should the lone arbitrator take an unreasonable position.

If you do request a hearing, you also can request a location that's more convenient than otherwise for you. Obviously it doesn't pay for an Oklahoma City investor to travel to New York to resolve a dispute over $1,000.

Your broker should respond to your claim within a month. If silence prevails, prodding the NASD is more likely than not to result in waking him or her up. If the NASD remains inactive, you'll have to keep calling the association or hire an attorney.

After you get a response from the brokerage firm, write to the firm, requesting certain documents—the individual broker's disciplinary history, and a record of all commissions received on transactions for your account. Also ask for the firm's compliance manual, which may in fact *prohibit* the types of trades made on your behalf.

Send a copy of your letter to the NASD, and keep pressing for a complete response. If necessary, write to the NASD Director of Arbitration, 33 Whitehall Street, New York, NY 10004. Also, call your state securities regulator and ask for the NASD's Central Registration Depository report on your broker. If you can show that the broker has a blemished past, you'll increase your chances for a recovery.

Eventually you'll be assigned an arbitration date and a list of arbitrators. Before consenting, ask the NASD for a summary of the arbitrators' past decisions. If you see one who consistently has favored the brokerage industry, insist upon a replacement. On average, over half of investors get an award in arbitration, generally amounting to about half of the losses they claim.

SUMMING UP

- Although most brokers are honest, there are many unscrupulous ones out there, working for large and small firms alike.
- Brokers earn commissions when you buy or sell securities, so they may urge you to trade more often than necessary, or to buy unsuitable investments; and they may even make false promises about the expected results.
- To protect yourself, make your goals clear to your broker, and monitor your statements regularly.
- *Don't* give your broker unrestricted authority to make trades on your account.
- As soon as you see signs of what might be improper behavior, complain emphatically to both your broker and the firm.
- If the situation isn't resolved, consult with an experienced securities lawyer.
- If your case is too small to interest an attorney, you can represent yourself in arbitration proceedings before the National Association of Securities Dealers.
- Before going to arbitration, get as much information as possible about both your transactions and your broker.

3

Pro Power

Finding a First-Class Investment Manager

Brokers aren't the only financial advisers who can rip you off. There are thousands of people calling themselves "financial planners" today, and they occupy a wide spectrum of ability and honesty. Some planners are hardworking, knowledgeable pros who perform a needed role, but others are incompetent or unscrupulous (or both). Reportedly, poor financial planning costs clients at least $300 million per year.

One twenty-four-year-old, for example, set himself up as a financial planner in Phoenix. He promised clients 4 percent–7 percent growth per *month* from stocks and commodities futures. Working a "Ponzi scheme," he used money from new investors to pay off old ones, build favorable word-of-mouth, and attract more money. By the time the whole venture collapsed, investors had lost over $5 million.

The message, of course, is to keep your expectations reasonable. If top money managers shoot for 12 percent or 15 percent annual returns, why should anyone be willing to promise you 50 percent or more?

17

Even if you avoid out-and-out rip-offs, you may fall prey to poor advice. That's what happened to Milton and Betty M., who took early retirement and moved to Florida. They consulted a "certified financial planner," who advised them to put almost $90,000 into limited partnerships and junk-bond funds.

The investments weren't washouts, but neither were they very good. After seven years, $90,000 had shrunk to $83,000—and that sum includes distributions received in that time frame. If Milton and Betty had simply kept their money in a bank account or money-market fund, they'd have had $130,000 or more.

Now, no one is saying you should put all of your money into bank accounts and money funds. For a fifty-five-year-old couple, growth is important—even critical. And, considering the strength of the stock and bond markets in the late 1980s and early 1990s, there were plenty of ways that growth could have been obtained.

Unfortunately, their "financial planner" didn't come up with a very good plan. So Milton and Betty had not only a sizable loss—they also had an even greater *opportunity cost*, the money they might have made but didn't.

Information, Please

How can you separate real financial planners from the scam artists and the second-raters? You can tell a lot from even your first meeting. If your planner recommends a particular investment right away, watch out. Chances are, every "plan" offered involves the same thing: life insurance or a deferred annuity or a growth-stock fund, on *any* of which the planner will collect a commission.

Because there's no perfect investment that's right for all clients, a good planner should ask you questions—lots of questions—before recommending *anything*. How old are you? How much do you earn? What assets do you have? What's your family situation? What are your goals? How comfortable are you with investments that can go down as well as up?

Only after you've answered these (and other) questions should the adviser come up with a thorough plan—insurance, tax planning, retirement planning, investing. He or she may even suggest ways to cut your spending so you'll be able to increase savings.

At this point, you probably *will* know whether you have a real planner or a commission-hungry salesperson. There's nothing wrong with buying financial products (or paying commissions for services rendered), but those products should make sense in the context of an *overall* plan.

The Checking Game

Before you waste time trying to discover who's a real planner and who isn't, here's a screening process you can use:

• *Find out if a planner is registered.* Planners usually must register with the federal Securities and Exchange Commission as well as with state regulators. If a planner can't show you proof of registration, ask why not. If that challenge doesn't bring the desired reaction, call the SEC (202-272-7450) *and* the state's securities department as soon as you can, to find out if that planner has ever been subjected to disciplinary actions or arbitration proceedings.

• *Check into a planner's educational and financial background.* A degree in finance, business, or economics *usually* is evidence of a basic understanding of money matters. Also, *most* bona fide planners have passed an exam to become a CPA (accounting), a chartered life underwriter or chartered financial consultant (both in life insurance), a certified financial planner, or a registered financial planner. Such credentials show *some* competence, although they are *not* guarantees of excellence in financial planning.

• *Ask how your planner will get paid.* A typical arrangement is fee-plus-commission. That is, you'll pay a fee for a plan, by the hour, or for an annual retainer. You'll also pay a commission for buying life insurance, mutual funds, and other products that the planner recommends. Some planners are "fee-only," but their fees tend to be higher than those charged by planners who accept commissions.

Fee-only planners portray themselves as unbiased, but the truth is that the world of financial advisers doesn't break down so neatly into saints and sinners. The important thing is full disclosure—you want to know exactly how much of your money goes to a planner, so you can decide whether he or she is worth it.

Take your own inclinations into account, too. If you're an active investor, the kind who likes to select stocks and mutual funds on your own, you don't need a commission-based planner who'll put you into mutual funds with a sales load: You can buy your own no-load funds.

But if you really want your planner to make all the decisions for you, such as picking specific mutual funds, you may be better off with a planner who'll do the work and receive a commission therefor.

• *Ask for references.* A good planner will have satisfied clients, those who have been relying on him or her for years. Get the names of some, and call to find out which services the planner has performed for them.

You also should ask the planner to show examples of plans he or she prepared in the past (with names deleted), along with follow-up reports. If each plan contains very similar recommendations, be cautious.

• *Use common sense.* One planner advised his clients, a married couple, to refinance their house, thereby increasing their mortgage from $17,000 to $90,000. Then he advised them to sell five blue-chip stocks, to raise another $80,000. The combined proceeds went into four limited partnerships and four mutual funds (with sales commissions for the planner).

Before going through with any such portfolio conversion, ask your planner for a written explanation of what all this is meant to accomplish. Chances are it won't seem as brilliant, in black and white, as it does when the planner is glibly promising you riches. If the scheme seems bizarre, back off.

Don't Swing at the First Pitch

You can't rely on federal or state regulators to help you find a first-class planner, or to bail you out after you've lost money due to following poor advice. You need to protect yourself by aggressively checking on a planner before making any commitment. It's a good idea to interview *at least* three planners, to see how their different styles compare, before making your decision. And always get information *in writing* before investing any money—*don't* proceed solely on what the planner recommends.

The same advice holds true when you're dealing with other types of financial pros, including brokers or insurance agents. Find out their backgrounds, check references, and get everything in writing. Interview several before *choosing* one. Before *trusting* any of them with your life's savings, think about whether his or her advice really makes sense for someone in your position.

SUMMING UP

• Virtually anyone can claim to be a financial planner, so expect to find frauds and incompetents as well as helpful professionals in that business.

• A real (genuine) financial planner will want to hear all about your personal situation before recommending a comprehensive course of action, whereas the second-raters will primarily want to sell you something ASAP.

• Always check on a financial planner via federal and state regulators.

• The really good planners probably will have an impressive educational background as well as professional credentials.

• Before you make any commitments, be sure to find out how your planner expects to get paid.

• Ask to see copies of prior financial plans for other clients, and check on a planner's record with existing clients.

• Follow the same strategy when choosing such other types of financial professionals as brokers and insurance agents.

4

If the Phone Rings, Hang Up

Protect Yourself From Telephone Scams

As bank-account and money-market fund interest rates fell during the late 1980s and early 1990s, investors became more and more hungry for higher yields. Sometimes even desperately so.

Take the case of Gale S., of Thousand Oaks, California. She's a real-estate agent, so she's not a financial babe-in-the-woods. Yet she couldn't resist the appeal of yields in the 12 percent–16 percent range pitched to her by phone.

Supposedly, her money was going into second mortgages arranged by mortgage brokers for homeowners and developers whose credit ratings couldn't meet bank lending standards. Why lend to risky borrowers? Because your loan is secured by the property. When you hold a second mortgage, your claim on the property comes right behind the first-mortgage holder's.

Unfortunately, Gale invested with Phillips Financial Group, also of Thousand Oaks. Some Phillips properties had not just two mortgages but *hundreds*, according to press reports. Some mortgages were even unrecorded, so investors were totally unprotected when the properties went into foreclosure. Gale, for example, discovered she was in 176th position! The commercial property securing her investment was valued at $800,000, yet total loans on this building were $3.6 million. So Gale wound up losing her $60,000 investment.

But Gale was not alone. Hundreds of investors may have lost an estimated total of $30 million in such investments sponsored by Phillips, according to the *Wall Street Journal.* Jackie L., for example (a Malibu teacher married to a retired airline pilot), reported that her family lost a total of $400,000. Two Phillips executives were sentenced to jail for grand theft—but that didn't compensate for their victims' losses in any meaningful way.

Crime Ring

Even if the perpetrators get caught, that's little consolation to the victims of telephone scams. A survey by Louis Harris & Associates, conducted for the National Consumers League, found that 92 percent of American households have been solicited on behalf of phone-fraud schemes. Yet only one-third of the fraud victims report the scams, and only a tenth ever get any of their money back. The way to protect yourself is to avoid being bilked in the first place.

It helps to be familiar with the ploys you'll hear from telemarketing frauds. Second-mortgage scams, for example, are popular in California because that state has a large legitimate second-mortgage business.

Farther east, in Ohio, "air-time" pitches prevail. Investors are told that they can buy time on cable and low-powered TV stations which would be resold to advertisers—mainly people selling gadgets. Naturally, investors are told that they can double their money in sixty days.

Just as naturally, the investors who believed in Vision Television of Wooster, Ohio, wound up losing $13 million, according to regulators. A Wayne County judge called Vision Television a massive fraud and sentenced its president to thirty-seven years in jail.

Not only are investors vulnerable to these air-time swindles; there also are bogus investments in cable TV, wireless-cable TV, and low-powered TV stations. Wireless cable, for example, is a microwave-based technology that allows cable TV to be distributed via a minimum of equipment.

The Federal Communications Commission holds periodic lotteries of wireless-cable licenses. Scam artists charge $5,000 and more to prepare lottery applications, even though winning is not guaranteed, but the potential victims don't know that. These application mills often churn out hundreds of applications for the same market. Plus, this "lottery" is for the opportunity to run a business, not for an automatic cash payout.

Wireless communications figure in yet another type of scam, according to federal regulators. Some deals offering participation in wireless-phone franchises are fraudulent; moreover, since they're structured as "limited liability companies" (LLCs), the organizers don't register the offerings with securities regulators, claiming instead that all of the investors are active managers in an operating company. Shielded from securities law, the sponsors may tell investors that the money is going into an operating wireless system with customers and all necessary FCC licenses, touting returns of 400 percent in three years. Of course, *no* legitimate investment would make such claims.

Dirty Little Secret

Some swindles are "silent." You might, for example, be told that you can get a great buy on Florida real estate, but must keep the deal secret for a year. The story is that the current owners have a "right of redemption," if they find out that their property is being sold. Of course, the real reason for the imposed secrecy is to allow promoters sufficient time to make their getaway.

Stock-market boiler-room scams can *really* make investors sweat. Some disreputable brokerage firms bring out "hot" new companies, selling their shares to the public. Using phone scripts, hundreds of brokers make thousands of calls a day promising huge profits. Investors have been known to part with thousands—even tens of thousands—of dollars. Usually, this money goes into the pockets of the brokers and company insiders. After the initial offering the company stumbles along, not posting meaningful profits, and the stock falls to a fraction of its offering price.

Not all telephone scams involve investments; other schemes can take your money just as rapidly. Consider what happened to Cliff B., an Oakland, California, sheet-metal worker facing a layoff. He was already behind in his rent, desperately looking for a loan. In a local newspaper, he saw an ad offering loans to people with no job and no credit history. He followed up with a call and was told by the voice on the phone that he could get a $5,000 bank loan at prevailing rates. The company running the ads would act as cosigner. He'd get his money within ten days.

The catch? Cliff had to pay $200 up front to cover processing costs. As you might have guessed, he paid his $200 and never saw a penny from the "loan company."

Loan scams are widespread, and so are phony credit-card deals. Callers with poor or no credit history are offered cards that are not MasterCard or Visa. In fact, they're not affiliated with *any* banks. All they do is allow you to buy merchandise out of an overpriced catalog, and even then you can expect to pay half the price in cash.

No Contest

Variations on the above theme are seemingly endless. For example, you may be told you've won a "guaranteed" prize in a contest. However, to get your prize you must send cash. One elderly victim borrowed the $600 she was told she needed to "register" the $37,000 prize she supposedly won. When her son went to visit, he found that she had no food in the house—she had sent all of her cash to the promoter, who was still promising a huge cash award.

Some contest scams tell you that in order to win, you must call a costly 900 phone number. To reduce the risk that consumers will catch on to the 900 game, some scams involve similar phone lines in the Dominican Republic (area code 809) or the Netherlands Antilles (599). Or, you might be charged for information provided on calls to an 800 line, and also asked to accept "long-distance charges" on what is really a toll-free line.

Charitable frauds are prevalent, too. Usually, the only "charity" involved is the caller.

Increasingly, con men are using advanced computer and telecommunications technology to find likely victims—often people who have been cheated before. Swindlers also can buy lists of callers to sex-talk and easy-credit 800 and 900 lines who are considered easy marks.

Incredibly, once isn't enough for some fraud victims. Some scam artists posing as investigators or attorneys or bonding agents get hold of the names of telemarketing victims and promise to help them get their money back. For a fee, of course. Victims become double victims. Dixie L., for example, lost $900 in a phone contest. Then a telemarketing firm told her it would help obtain a refund. The seventy-four-year-old woman paid $670 in "investigative fees"; but the only help she received was a letter advising her to call the local state attorney general's office.

A new wave of telephone frauds aims to tap people who want to be caring and compassionate. In 1994, for example, the Attorney General of Massachusetts brought a suit against the National Awareness Foundation, which was raising money under the name "Hugs Not Drugs." The money was supposed to distribute workbooks in elementary schools, but neither funds nor books were distributed, according to state officials. Before you give money to *any* cause, no matter *how* worthy it sounds, *always* ask to see something in writing.

Pull the Plug

The best way to protect yourself against phone fraud is to hang up whenever *anybody* calls you and asks for money. You'll never lose a penny, and you'll save a lot of time you'd waste listening to come-ons. However, since some legitimate brokers, insurance agents, and financial planners also use the phone as a prospecting tool, you could be passing up an opportunity for genuine financial assistance by cutting them off too soon.

One way to tell the difference is to call 800-876-7060, a hotline sponsored by the National Consumers League in Washington, D.C. The people answering the phone can help you to evaluate proposals and steer you away from blatant frauds. Another resource you can use is your local Better Business Bureau. Call the BBB before making any purchases, to find out if there have been complaints registered against either the company or its management.

Better yet, use your own common sense to screen out scams. Whenever you hear extravagant promises, forget the deal. There's *no* investment guaranteed to double your money in sixty days. Be especially leery if there's some time pressure to send in money because the opportunity "won't last."

Always ask for something on paper before sending money. You can't really understand *any* investment from only a few sentences over the phone. Ask for something you can read at your leisure, such as a prospectus, in order to compare the risks with the potential rewards. If you're not comfortable with financial documents, ask for help from a friend or adviser you trust.

Ask for references, too: A legitimate financial professional will invariably work with a bank, a CPA, an attorney. Get names, and find out how long the people bearing them have been working with your caller. In other words, do your homework. Do everything you can to find out if this is a venture in which you want to get involved, and a person or group with whom you want to do business.

Even if all your investigations come up positive, crawl before you walk. *Don't* invest your life's savings in any one deal, no matter *how* alluring it seems. Invest a small amount, then see how things progress. You always can put more money in, if you're pleased—but it's nearly impossible to get money back after you've been ripped off.

SUMMING UP

• Almost all Americans are exposed to telephone scams. Victims rarely get their money back.

• Investment scams include second mortgages, hot stocks, TV systems, and TV air-time.

• Perhaps the most prevalent swindle in the U.S. today is the loan scam, requiring you to pay up-front fees in return for credit.

• Before you send any money to a voice you know only on the phone, check with organizations such as the National Consumers League and the Better Business Bureau.

• Do your own homework, looking carefully into both the legitimacy of the deal and the people offering it to you.

Part II

Natural
(and Unnatural)
Disasters

5

On the House

Protecting Your Home Against Fire, Theft, and Vandals

After Hurricane Andrew tore across Florida, creating a record $16.5 billion in damages, thousands of people ruefully inspected the wreckage of what used to be their homes. Other recent front-page disasters have included floods in the Midwest and fires and earthquakes in California. Everyone who buys homeowners insurance should learn a lesson from others' misfortunes.

Insurance should *really* be insurance: Buy protection against a *worst-case* scenario. Only after you're covered for catastrophes should you worry about whether to buy insurance for damage to your lawnmower and your CD player.

The most important question is how much insurance to buy. The answer: as much as it would cost to rebuild your house if it's completely wiped out. But *don't* buy insurance to cover the cost of your land. (Homeowners insurance should include liability, too, as described in Chapter 24.)

Shop for "replacement-cost" coverage, *not* "actual cash-value" coverage, because the latter pays replacement cost *minus* depreciation. In case of a natural disaster, actual cash-value coverage may fall far short of the amount needed to replace your house. As Hurricane Andrew demonstrated, your home might be totally destroyed in a major storm. In any case, you should insure your house for at least 80 percent of estimated market value—otherwise, your policy might not pay you in full for replacement.

Some policies state that they will *upgrade to code*. In Florida, for example, there were stories of houses put together with tacks; upgrade-to-code policies would pay for whatever screws or nails are required. Many localities now insist that destroyed homes be rebuilt to tougher, more expensive building-code standards. A variation on code policies, sold by many insurers, is "guaranteed replacement-cost" coverage, which pays to replace losses, no matter what the upper limits of the policy.

However, for many insurers, replacement cost excludes expenses for complying with building standards that did not exist when the home was built. For example, Charles P., a homeowner in Saga Bay, Florida, whose home suffered heavy damage from Hurricane Andrew, found that it had to be raised several feet to comply with new rules on flood plains. Even though Charles received $120,000 from his replacement-cost policy, he had to spend an additional $50,000 to raise his home. So always ask your insurance agent what your exposure would be to building-code-related expenses, and how much extra you'd have to pay for full coverage.

Don't buy insurance based on either what you paid for your house or what it might sell for today. Instead, insure against the cost of *completely* rebuilding it. That should include the cost of demolishing any wreckage left on-site, and carting the rubble to a dump. To get an estimate of probable rebuilding cost, ask a local bank for the name of a reliable appraiser. Underinsurance can be a problem in areas where inflation has driven up housing costs. Many of the homes destroyed in the Oakland Hills and southern California fires were inadequately insured.

The Cutting Edge

Full catastrophic coverage, of course, will cost more than partial coverage. If you can't afford to pay top dollar, don't skimp on the amount of protection you buy. Instead, take a higher deductible.

The standard deductible in a homeowners policy is $250. As a rough guideline, you can cut your premiums 5 percent–10 percent by choosing a $500 deductible. A policy with a $1,000 deductible will cost about 15 percent less than one with a $250 deductible, and going from a $50 to a $1,000 deductible can knock more than 40 percent off your annual premiums. With a higher deductible, you'll pay for $500 or $1,000 worth of damage but leave the insurance company on the hook in case of a disaster. That's the fundamental idea behind buying insurance.

You'll probably wind up ahead with a higher deductible. In 1993, one major insurer quoted a price of $746 per year to insure a $250,000 house on Long Island, near New York City. That policy would have a $250 deductible and provide up to $200,000 (80 percent) coverage. However, if the deductible were increased to $1,000, the annual premium would fall to $526 per year. What's more, if the deductible is maintained at $1,000, coverage could be increased to 100 percent and the annual premium would be only $675, considerably less than the cost of the $250-deductible, 80 percent-coverage policy.

Besides increasing deductibles, you also should install good burglar- and fire-alarm systems. You can get discounts on premiums up to 15 percent from many insurance companies. Add a fire-sprinkler system and your discount may go up to 30 percent. Additional discounts may be available to senior citizens, owners of new homes, and nonsmokers.

What sort of disasters should you insure against? The basic homeowners policy, HO1, covers damages from wind, fire, rain, lightning, explosions, and riots, the most likely causes of disasters. (In coastal areas, you may have to buy separate wind and hail coverage.)

Increasingly, state regulators are phasing out HO1 in favor of HO2 and HO3, which are broader. These latter policies also cover most other major hazards, such as leaks from frozen pipes, and damage from snow on your roof. Especially if you live in an area that suffers from cold winters, it's worth pricing the extra coverage.

Recommendation: Ask your agent to quote you prices for "all-perils" or "all-risk" policies, as opposed to the standard "named-perils" policy. The latter protects you against *specific* risks—vandalism, additional living expenses in case your house can't be occupied—while all-perils policies cover everything *except* risks specifically excluded, such as floods, earthquakes, war, and nuclear accidents.

One upstate New York homeowner, for example, had an unexpected visitor during his absence: a deer, which came and went through picture windows, stomped the furniture, and kicked holes in the walls. The $10,000 loss was *covered* in his all-perils policy, whereas a named-perils policy would have *excluded* it. All-perils policies may also cover chemical and paint spills, breakage, lock replacement, blood stains, and scorching without fire—all of which may be excluded by a named-perils policy.

If you rent, you should have basic tenants insurance, known as HO4, because your landlord's insurance won't cover your property. Depending on where you live, a policy covering $25,000 worth of possessions will cost $75 to $225 per year, with a $250 deductible.

No Day at the Beach

Some insurers are cutting back on coverage, particularly in waterfront areas. If you own a vacation house on the beach, or are shopping for one, you need to know the cost and availability of insuring it.

So far, Florida has been the hardest hit. At least twenty companies, including Allstate and Prudential, have announced plans to reduce their presence in Florida or pull out altogether. Many companies are avoiding Hawaii, while some are backing away from Northeastern coastal areas and Texas. On Long Island, for example, more than fifty insurance companies have stopped accepting new customers within 1,000 feet of the shore, while some companies won't sell insurance within 5,000 feet of the shoreline.

That doesn't mean you won't be able to buy homeowners insurance if you have beachfront property, however. You'll likely be able to get it from a company that has remained in the market, or from a state pool. However, you'll certainly pay dearly for the coverage. In Massachusetts, for instance, premiums in the state-run association can be 60 percent higher than the cost of private insurance.

For beachfront property owners, higher prices for insurance pack a *double* wallop. Not only will you have greater out-of-pocket costs each year, but also, higher insurance rates will lower the resale value of your home. For prospective property owners, the cost of buying insurance should be factored into other expenses (taxes, maintenance) before deciding how much to bid. In many coastal areas, you'll likely need to have homeowners insurance lined up in advance, in order to obtain a mortgage.

Besides buying the right kind of insurance, there are other steps you should take to preserve your waterfront property. Hire a reputable inspector to check on construction before you buy. (You can do the same for property you already own.) If there are structural flaws, see if they can be repaired economically.

A knowledgeable, reputable agent can help you buy the homeowners insurance you really need—no more, no less. Yes, there are agents like that, but you may have to search hard, asking friends for recommendations, before you find such an exemplar of intelligence and integrity. That's especially true if you're a condo owner: You'll likely need a savvy agent to tell you how much you can rely upon the condo association's policy, and how much individual coverage you'll need as a supplement.

USAA and Amica were the two top-rated homeowners insurers in a recent *Consumer Reports* survey of customer satisfaction; and USAA and State Farm have high levels of consumer satisfaction, according to complaint studies by state insurance departments. To check on an insurer, ask your state's department how it compares in terms of complaints versus complaints against other insurers of similar size. In addition, look for companies with good ratings from A. M. Best, Duff & Phelps, Moody's, and Standard & Poor's.

In 1994, a new type of homeowners insurance came to the market—*perpetual* insurance, sold by companies such as Mutual Assurance, Cincinnati Equitable, Baltimore Equitable, and Philadelphia Contributorship. With these policies, you pay one large lump sum up front. Say that your annual homeowner's premium presently is $500: You will pay (say) $5,000 to the insurer in one shot, and make *no* further payments. And your premium won't be increased unless you want more coverage.

You're effectively getting a 10 percent return on your money if you pay $5,000 and save a $500 premium each year. And if you sell your home or cancel your insurance, your deposit will be refunded. (Home buyers might want to increase their mortgage by $5,000 or so, using the extra money to pay for a perpetual policy.)

Beyond the Limits

Homeowners policies don't cover floods or earthquakes. If you live in a region that's vulnerable to earthquakes, you can buy appropriate coverage as an *endorsement* (added feature) to your homeowners policy. In California, where earthquake insurance is sold separately, insurers are required to offer it to residents every other year.

This coverage is expensive in quake-prone areas, even with high deductibles—which usually run to 2 percent–10 percent of the policy's limit. Lisa F., of Sherman Oaks, California, for example, paid $775 per year for $700,000 worth of earthquake insurance, with a 5 percent deductible. She suffered $50,000 worth of damage in the earthquake that struck southern California in 1994, and had to pay the first $35,000 worth of damages (5 percent of $700,000). Thus, her recovery was limited to $15,000. Joel G., of that state's Las Feliz, suffered $20,000 worth of damage in that quake, but recovered only about $5,000 because he had to pay the first $15,000 (10 percent of his $150,000 policy limit).

If your home was built recently and is bolted to the foundation, you may be able to reduce earthquake insurance costs by reducing coverage, taking a chance that your home won't be completely wiped out. If Joel had owned a $100,000 policy instead of a $150,000 policy, for example, he would have paid a smaller premium and collected $10,000, instead of $5,000.

Stinging From the Rain

Flood insurance is different from earthquake insurance. Coverage is available through the federal government's National Flood Insurance Program. However, you can buy flood insurance *only* if your community elects to participate in a program involving taking steps to reduce local flood dangers.

Although flood insurance is provided by the federal government, it's sold through agents affiliated with private insurance companies. If you suffer flood damage, you'll have to work with the company's reps to collect on claims. (Your standard homeowners policy, while it *won't* cover coastal or stream flooding, *should* cover water damage caused by heavy rains.)

Over 18,000 communities participate in the national flood insurance program. If you own property in these communities you're eligible to buy it; indeed, many mortgage lenders *require* you to carry it. Coverage is capped at $185,000 for the house, and another $60,000 for its contents.

Costs for flood insurance vary, depending on the house's location, age, and construction. If your house is above likely flood levels and built according to current standards, you might pay only a few hundred dollars a year. On the other hand, premiums for a high-risk house might cost $5,000 and up. Deductibles typically are $500–$750. Prices also will vary depending on how much your community has done to mitigate the risk of flooding. For information on the national flood insurance program, call 800-638-6620.

Since 1991 (and at least until the time this book went to press), Congress has attempted to pass new flood insurance legislation. Proposed legislation would require the Federal Emergency Management Agency to map thirty-year and sixty-year erosion zones. *No* federal flood insurance would be available for new buildings in the thirty-year zone, and insurance would be *limited* for new buildings in the sixty-year zone.

Existing structures would be eligible for federal flood insurance, but premium increases would be huge. Financial institutions would be prohibited from making loans unless flood insurance was in place. Owners would be allowed to buy private insurance, but such coverage, if available, would likely be quite expensive. If you're shopping for waterfront property, be aware that the cost of flood insurance might rise to scary heights within the next few years.

Taking a Rider

Besides buying insurance to protect your home, you'll also want to cover the contents. Replacing furnishings, appliances, and so on could add up to almost as much as replacing the house. Most homeowners policies set limits for what they'll pay to replace personal possessions—typically 50 percent–75 percent of the coverage on the house itself. For valuables such as furs, jewelry, and silver, you'll probably need separate policies ("floaters").

The more documentation you have regarding your possessions, the better will your insurance company be able to handle your claim. You might photograph your property in your home, with a still or video camera, and make up a floor plan of your house, showing where things are located. *Keep copies* of any films or maps or lists *off-premises*, so they won't be destroyed in case of disaster. A safe-deposit box may be the ideal place.

Here's a recommendation: Software packages for personal computers are increasingly popular. Personal Record Keeper and My-Treasures contain inventory programs. They organize your possessions by types and units and worth of furniture, appliances, collectibles, and so on. These programs will ask whether an item was bought or inherited, how much it cost, its replacement value, etc. Again, *keep a copy* of your computerized inventory *off-premises*.

Whatever your recording system, note the make, model, and serial number of every item whenever possible. Save your receipts (especially for expensive purchases). And update your list after every major purchase!

If you take these advance precautions, you'll be able to *prove* what you've lost. Your claim will will be processed more rapidly than otherwise, and you're more likely to collect in full. For more information on homeowners insurance, a free brochure, "Insurance for Your House and Personal Possessions," is available from the Insurance Information Institute, 110 William Street, New York, NY 10038. The Institute also runs a toll-free hotline (800-942-4242) to answer questions on homeowners insurance.

A Pound of Prevention

To *really* protect your possessions, take every possible step to keep thieves from seeing your home as an easy target. Make it difficult for burglars to break into your home. You can't totally burglar-proof your house, but you can get close to doing so. Here's how:

• Leave a radio or TV on when your house is empty. Automatic timers can turn lights on or off at irregular times while no one is home.

• If you're going on vacation, have someone pick up newspapers, shovel snow, and the like.

• Don't stop your daily newspapers, mail, garbage, recycling pick-ups, etc., when you're away from home, because such stop notices will be posted at the service providers' premises. Instead, ask friends or neighbors to pick up your mail and newspapers.

• Install outside lighting near all doors and windows. For $10–$20 apiece, you can buy photoelectric cells that turn outside lights on at dusk (and whenever else darkness occurs), and off at dawn (and at other times of equal natural illumination). Motion sensors can be hooked up to doorway lights, or to floodlights under the eaves.

• Post a sign warning that your house is protected by an alarm system. The sign can go by the front door, with copies at the back and on the sides.

• Put dog paraphernalia (water dish, large rawhide bone) outside by the back door, whether or not you have a dog.

• Join a Neighborhood Watch program sponsored by your local police. Such groups keep their eyes out for criminal activity in the neighborhood.

• Use metal or solid-core wood doors that open into the house, so hinges aren't exposed. If you have doors with outdoor hinges, get nonremovable pins from a hardware store.

• If you have a glass panel in a door, or a glass window near a door, replace the glass with an unbreakable material, or install a decorative grill over the panel.

• Install on all entry doors a deadbolt lock that operates with a key from the outside and a knob on the inside. Your dead bolt locks should have reinforced strike plates using 3-inch screws.

• Wedge sliding doors and windows shut; install metal pins on double-hung windows. A metal "Charley bar" that costs less than $10 spans the gap between the interior slider and the frame of a sliding door.

• Keep bushes trimmed below window level to expose would-be burglars.

• Install a chain lock and/or one-way, wide-angle "peep hole" viewer on your front door.

• Use an electric, self-locking garage-door opener, and put a lock on any door from your garage to your house. Put a heavy-duty padlock through the track just above the garage-door roller, in case burglars figure out how to bypass the electric opener.

• Keep your garage door closed at all times possible, and cover garage windows so nobody can see if your car is inside.

• Lock jewelry and valuables in a drawer, cabinet, or safe. Fire-resistant safes are not necessarily burglar-proof because they're made of light-gauge steel. For full protection, buy one made from steel and concrete. Such a safe, with one to three cubic feet of interior capacity, might sell for up to $350. Put it in a closet and anchor it to the floor.

• Install a home security alarm system that will be triggered by *any* tampering with doors or windows. A "central station" system transmits the alarm to a twenty-four-hour security staff, who will notify the police.

According to a Temple University study, having an alarm makes it nearly four times less likely you'll be hit. ADT Security Systems (800-238-4636) and Brinks Home Security (800-227-4657) offer basic systems that cost around $200 to install, plus $20–$25 per month for central-station monitoring. Wireless systems can cost as much as

$1,000—but with one of those systems, you won't have to drill holes and run wires all over your house.

Here's another recommendation: There are times when extra vigilance is needed. Professional burglars, for example, read wedding and death notices, then strike while you're out attending the service. If you're facing such a situation, make sure your alarm system is on, and ask a neighbor to keep an eye on your house. Hire a guard if you're particularly concerned.

Today, nearly 90 percent of all break-ins go unsolved. On average, burglars get away with over $1,000 worth of cash and valuables. A relatively few dollars spent on basic burglar-proofing now can spare you expensive losses in the future.

What's more, a few dollars spent today may also help you get your property back tomorrow. For example, Tom and Carol M. of Great Falls, Virginia, pay $6 a month to have a caller ID box connected to their home phone. Caller ID keeps a log of incoming calls, including the phone numbers from which they have been placed. When Tom and Carol came home from a vacation, they found that more than $10,000 worth of coins, stamps, and jewelry had been stolen. They checked the caller ID records, on the theory that a burglar might have been casing their house, and discovered several late-night calls from an unfamiliar phone number. The police followed up and found the phone calls were made by a young man in the neighborhood. He confessed, and Tom and Carol got back most of the stolen goods.

SUMMING UP

• Homeowners insurance should protect you from a castrophe that totally destroys your house—or nearly wrecks it.
• Policies should provide enough coverage to replace your house, upgrading to code if necessary, if disaster strikes.
• An all-perils policy will cover you for most occurences, even if such are not specifically cited in the policy.
• To cut the costs of catastrophic coverage, increase your deductible to $500 or $1,000.
• Policy discounts may be available for such various beneficial details as alarm systems, new homes, senior citizens, and nonsmokers.
• Special coverage is necessary to protect against earthquakes and floods.

• You can protect household possessions with extra insurance, called *riders*, especially if you maintain a thorough inventory of the items in your home.

• Always make sure your house appears occupied, and install safety devices to keep out intruders.

• Caller ID not only protects you against crank calls, but can indicate and record the phone number of a burglar who has been casing and calling your house.

6

Car Wars

Buying Auto Insurance That Won't Drive You Bankrupt

One or two thousand dollars—or even more—for auto insurance each year may seem like a lot, and in fact *is*. But suppose your car cost you $25,000 or more. Not many years ago, you could have bought a small *house* for that much. So it makes good sense to protect such a valuable asset.

In addition, when you drive your car (or another family member does), a potentially lethal weapon is put into operation. Should tragedy strike, and your car kill or injure someone, you could lose everything you own—unless you have the proper insurance.

So buying auto insurance is serious business, indeed. On the other hand, you don't need to buy the most expensive coverage just because your agent recommends it. Often, some aspect or another of insurance coverage is either redundant or unnecessary. If you know where to cut back, you can save hundreds of dollars a year, yet still enjoy full protection.

Playing Geography

There's one sure way to beat the cost of auto insurance: move. Insuring a Ford Taurus in Indiana might cost $750–$800 per year, as opposed to $1,500 in New York, and over $2,000 in Los Angeles. However, you may not want to live in Indiana, or be able to make a living there. You can, though, choose a car that's relatively inexpensive to insure. Typically, family-oriented, four-door cars such as the Taurus, Buick Century, Chevrolet Lumina, Oldsmobile Cutlass, and Pontiac Grand Prix cost a lot less to insure than the likes of the Chevrolet Camaro, Ford Mustang, and Pontiac Firebird.

Whether they're driving a Taurus in Topeka or a Camaro in Chicago, safe drivers pay less for auto insurance. The more moving violations you incur, and the more accidents in which you're involved, the faster you'll be downgraded from a "preferred" to a "standard" to a "nonstandard" risk. The lower your rating, the higher the premium you'll have to pay.

At some point, if your record continues to deteriorate, you may not be able to buy commercial insurance at all. If that happens, you may have to buy auto insurance from a state insurance pool, where your premium might be 300 percent higher than what "preferred" drivers pay. *So drive carefully.* And *don't* report minor accidents: The amount of your reimbursement likely will be less than you'll pay in higher premiums over the years!

More important, the benefits of safe driving go well beyond lower insurance premiums. When you avoid accidents, you protect yourself and your family. So *buckle up, keep within the speed limits,* and *don't drive after drinking.* Too, learn how to *correctly* operate your vehicle. For example: If you have antilock brakes, don't pump them when you skid—the proper technique is to apply steady pressure to the brake pedal and let the antilock system take over.

Moreover, you might want to consider "crashworthiness" when you choose a car. When the National Highway Traffic Safety Administration graded 1994 models, the Chevrolet Camaro and the Ford Bronco got top marks in test crashes into fixed barriers at thirty-five miles per hour. Both drivers and passengers had less than a 10 percent chance of being seriously injured, assuming they were wearing seat belts.

Shop Around

First, you should settle on exactly what kind of auto insurance you need—and on nothing beyond that. Then, get phone bids from several different insurers. When you do shop for coverage, here's what you should concentrate on:

• *Liability insurance.* The key coverage here is *bodily injury liability*, insurance that will pay medical expenses and legal fees for anyone hurt in an accident where you're at fault. At minimum, you should be covered up to $100,000 per person and $300,000 per accident.

You'll also need *property damage liability* coverage, which will pay for repairs on a vehicle you hit. Today, $10,000 in property liability coverage may not be enough—you probably should carry at least $50,000 worth.

Indeed, the basic liability coverage is known as 100/300/50, which is handy when you're comparison-shopping. However, if your net worth is over $300,000, you might want to increase liability coverage to $200,000 per person and $500,000 per accident. Usually, the cost of the added coverage is modest.

• *Collision and comprehensive insurance.* This coverage pays for damage to your own car, as well as for fire and theft. You're better off if you buy "pure" insurance: Protect against a catastrophe, but pay for your own *minor* repairs. In other words, take a higher deductible and pay a lower premium.

You might, for example, pay $350 per year to buy collision insurance, if you choose a $100 deductible. Raise that deductible to $500 and you might pay $250 per year. You save $100 per year by agreeing to pay for repairs up to $500. Similar savings can be achieved by taking a $500 or even a $1,000 deductible on comprehensive insurance, which covers theft and natural disasters.

Another way to cut insurance costs is to drop all collision coverage if your car is over five years old and collision insurance exceeds 10 percent of the car's value. If your car is worth less than $2,500, for example, why pay $250 per year for collision coverage? If your car is wrecked, buy a new one.

Moreover, even if you pay for insurance, you might not be able to collect. Most insurers won't cover a car for more than it's worth; they won't pay $5,000 worth of damages on a car worth $2,500. So get the "book value" of your old car from an auto dealer or your insurance agent, and drop the coverage when it's no longer worthwhile. Publications such as the *Blue Book* also will have this information.

• *Uninsured motorist coverage.* Do you really need this insurance, which kicks in only if you have an accident with a driver who's at fault *and* who doesn't have auto insurance? Some experts advocate buying it, while others say it merely duplicates your own health and liability insurance. *Our* position is to buy it, but don't go overboard—don't spend more than, say, $50 per year, for which you should be able to get $100,000 worth of coverage.

Where to Apply the Brakes

The coverages mentioned so far are those you'll need to protect your car(s) and your personal assets. Beyond them, there are a lot of coverages that you probably *don't* need:

• *Medical-payments insurance.* This coverage pays medical expenses when someone named in your policy or riding in your car is injured in an auto accident. Skip this coverage: Family members should be covered by health insurance, while liability insurance will pay for other people.

• *No-fault, or personal-injury protection (PIP).* In some states, this coverage for medical expenses, lost wages, etc., is optional. If so, decline it, because it duplicates other coverages you should have.

• *Miscellaneous coverages.* Adding coverage for road service, stolen audio equipment, car rentals if you can't use your own, and so on can drive up your insurance bill. In truth, these aren't such potential catastrophes that you should insure against them.

• *Extended-service contracts.* Auto dealers often push these contracts that will provide service for up to five years. But this insurance is expensive (as much as $1,200), and the problems it covers seldom appear in the first few years of ownership.

Dialing for Dollars

After you have decided which coverage you want and don't want, call *at least five* insurers and ask for quotes on this insurance—no more and no less. The spread between the highest and lowest quotes may be several hundred dollars per year—even as much as $1,000! To get quotes, call some independent agents, as well as companies (such as State Farm, Nationwide, and Amica) that sell directly to consumers.

Don't forget to ask for discounts, which can be quite sizable in auto insurance:

• *Out-of-towners.* If any child of yours is a college student who doesn't take your car to school, you're entitled to a discount.

• *Senior citizens.* Depending on the state and the company, drivers over age fifty may get 20 percent discounts.

• *Crime stoppers.* Discounts may be available if you install an alarm or some type of disabling device (see below).

• *Driver ed.* If you have—or a family member has—successfully completed a driver-education or defensive-driving course, you may be entitled to a discount of up to 15%.

• *Smoke out.* Some companies give discounts for nonsmokers.

• *Packaged deals.* Insuring both your house and your car with the same company may knock as much as 25 percent off your rate.

• *No-fault.* In about one-third of the states, you can cut your liability insurance premiums by up to 20 percent if you pass up your right to sue.

Also, some states *require* you to buy no-fault or PIP insurance, which covers your medical bills and at least *some* lost wages. If your health insurance company agrees to be the primary payer for these medical bills, you can cut PIP costs up to 40 percent. If you have an option, choose the highest possible deductible for PIP, which will reduce your cost.

For a free booklet, "Understanding Your Auto Insurance Policy and Get the Most for Your Money," send a stamped, self-addressed No. 10 envelope to The Society of Chartered Property and Casualty Underwriters, 720 Providence Road, P.O. Box 3309, Malvern, PA 19355-0709.

Stop, Thief!

Another way to cut auto insurance costs is to take crime-prevention measures: There's a car theft in the U.S. every twenty seconds. According to the latest available statistics (1992), 1.6 million cars were stolen in that year. Auto theft is increasing particularly fast in medium-sized suburbs (those with populations of 100,000 to 200,000).

Auto theft creates a huge expense for auto insurers—so they're willing to give you a discount if you take steps to foil car thieves. Discounts range from 5 percent to 35 percent of your policy's comprehensive insurance. Some states (New York and Texas, for example) require insurers to give discounts if certain anti-theft devices are installed.

Take the case of Al and Judy, a married couple in their thirties who live in Brooklyn and own a 1993 Ford Taurus. They pay $1,232 per year for comprehensive coverage from Aetna.

• They can etch the vehicle ID number onto their car windows, to facilitate the vehicle's return, at a cost of around $60. Aetna will in return give them a 5 percent discount—*more* than $60 per year.

• They can buy an alarm system with an "ignition killer" for about $300. The discount from Aetna would be 10 percent–15 percent, about $120–$180 per year, depending on whether the system is switched on manually (lower discount) or automatically. Established companies such as Excalibur, Alpine, Clifford Electronics, Crime-stopper, Directed Electronics, and Audiovox offer lifetime warranties.

• They can buy an electronic tracking system, such as LoJack, Code-Alarm, or PacTel's Teletrac, all of which cost $600 and up. Again, Aetna would offer a 15 percent discount, which means over $180 per year off the insurance bill.

If Al and Judy install multiple anti-theft devices, Aetna will give discounts of up to 25 percent (over $300) per year.

Although Aetna gives no discount for steering-wheel bar locks, such as The Club, *some* insurers will give a 5 percent discount. These bars usually cost $20–$75. Not only do anti-theft precautions lower your auto insurance premiums; they also help you to avoid the expense and aggravation of having your car stolen.

You can insist upon anti-theft protection when you buy a new car. General Motors, for example, has a PASS-KEY system, in which a microchip embedded in the ignition key must match a code in an on-board computer before the car will start. For some GM models, the car-theft rate has dropped sharply since PASS-KEY was introduced.

No matter how much or how little you spend on anti-theft devices, don't ignore some basic precautions, the principal one of which is: *Always lock your car and take your keys with you.* Half of all stolen cars aren't locked, and one in five has a key in the ignition!

Peter Dickinson, editor of *The Retirement Letter*, offers these other tips for thwarting auto thieves:

• *Have your car dealer or locksmith punch out the ID numbers printed on your car keys so they can't be easily duplicated.* Keep your own record of those numbers in a safe place.

• *Keep a spare set of car keys in your wallet.* Don't put spare keys in one of those magnetic boxes that fasten to metal car parts, because thieves look for them—and find them.

• *Conceal car stereo equipment, cellular phones, radar detectors, etc.* Black cardboard taped over the dashboard can be effective. You also can buy a "Lasso Lock" that wraps around and secures stereo equipment.

• *Buy gas-tank locks and interior hood locks for further protection.*

Rent Checks

If you rent cars, watch out. Historically, your auto insurance would travel with you when you rented a car. Carless big-city residents (for example) who carried *no* auto insurance could nevertheless rely on the rental company's coverage. But increasing costs have caused cutbacks—often at *your* expense. Today your personal auto insurance may *not* apply to rental cars, and the car-rental company may not offer built-in coverage, either.

So check before you rent a car. Ask your agent if your auto insurance applies to rentals, and if you're employed by a sizable organization, find out whether your employer's insurance will cover your business rentals. If you *don't* carry auto insurance, check to see whether your homeowners or excess liability (*umbrella*) coverage will protect you.

If you find out your coverage *won't* cover auto rentals, there nevertheless are a few steps you can take. For example, you can use a major credit card to rent from a major car-rental company: American Express cards or Gold Visa or MasterCard often will provide collision insurance. For liability coverage, though, you may have to spend an extra $5–10 per day to buy special insurance when you rent the car.

Be especially careful when you rent outside the United States or Canada, because most auto insurance policies won't reach that far. Try to rent in advance, preferably through a knowledgeable travel agent—and buy whatever auto insurance is necessary.

The Fix Is In

Whether your car has been in an accident or needs repairs for some other reason, you have to be careful about getting your car fixed. You can easily wind up overpaying, with your car *still* not running well.

Your safest bet is to take your car to an independent repair shop, rather than to your dealership—because independents tend to charge less (as much as 50 percent less). The only exception might be in case of a problem that only a dealer would know how to handle, such as a flaw in your car's electronic dashboard.

Whenever you can, talk directly to the mechanic who'll be working on your car. If you talk to the manager who talks to the clerk who writes up the repair order, chances are your message will lose something in the translation. When you speak to the mechanic yourself, you can be more sure than otherwise that he or she really understands the problem.

In a way, getting your car repaired is like seeing a doctor or a lawyer: You want to be sure you're working with a reputable professional. So get references, and mention your mutual contact's name when you call for your first appointment. If you find a mechanic you can rely upon, especially long-term, you'll avoid the scams that unfortunately are too common in the auto repair industry.

SUMMING UP

- Auto insurance rates vary widely, with the highest prices often found in urban areas of the Northeast and California.
- There's a great variance in rates from one model of car to another, with family-type cars often costing less to insure.
- No matter where or what you drive, a record without accidents or moving violations is vital to maintaining low insurance premiums.
- You need to carry liability insurance amply covering both people and cars you might injure in an accident.
- Collision insurance is important with a new car, but increasingly less so as it ages and loses value.
- Raising your deductibles can cut your costs for collision insurance.
- Once you have liability, collision, and comprehensive insurance, other coverage may not be necessary.
- Call several different agents for bids before buying insurance, mentioning all the factors that entitle you to discounts.
- If you install anti-theft devices, you can reduce your insurance bill while you deter would-be thieves.
- Before renting a car, check to see if you need to buy additional insurance coverage on it.

7

When You Buy Big, Buy Right

Keep High-Priced Lemons Out of Your Shopping Cart

A hurricane can rip the roof right off your house (or the house off its foundation). A burglar can snatch your irreplaceable jewelry. And you can also suffer a huge house-related loss by purchasing the wrong home at the wrong price.

When you're shopping for a house, don't rush. Take a good look to see what's on the market, and what the asking prices are. Then, when you find a house you like, make a bid lower than the asking price. *Then* negotiate. Chances are, both parties will meet halfway between push and shove.

But your greatest risk isn't that you'll pay a few thousand dollars more than you might have, had you done sharper negotiating. Your house may truly become a money pit if it needs extensive repairs that you hadn't bargained on. So hire a professional inspector to look at the place, after your bid has been accepted. If you don't know of an inspector, your mortgage lender probably does. Inspectors affiliated with the American Society of Home Inspectors are required to pass qualifying exams, and should be expected to have enough professional experience to match their marks.

Typically, an inspection will cost less than $300. For that, you should get a written report and follow-up recommendations. You're better off spending the money on an inspection rather than relying upon—or buying—a home warranty, which may prove of little value in case you later have huge repair expenses. (A home warranty is a nice "throw-in" when you're buying a house, but you shouldn't pay extra for one. If a warranty *is* included, you're better off if it's backed by an independent warrantor rather than by the builder, who may not be around to honor it.)

Dealing With Defects

Your inspection may turn up only minor flaws, or it may reveal serious water damage, termites, and so on. In the latter case, reconsider whether you really want the house. At the least, reduce your offering price significantly, or insist that the seller pay for any needed repairs before the house changes hands. If the seller performs the repairs, the "fixed" items should be reinspected.

Make sure your inspector checks for radon, an odorless, cancer-causing gas found in unsafe concentrations in about 12 percent of U.S. houses, according to the federal Environmental Protection Agency (EPA). Besides the health risk, high levels of radon will reduce the resale value of your home. Excess radon levels generally can be corrected for $500–$2,500. The EPA publishes a "Home Buyer's and Seller's Guide to Radon," which costs $1.50 from the U.S. Government Printing Office, Superintendent of Documents, P.O. Box 371954, Pittsburgh, PA 15250 (202-783-3238). Ask for stock number 055-000-00428-5.

More prevalent than radon is lead-based paint, found in potentially dangerous levels in about 75 percent of homes built before 1980, the U.S. Department of Housing and Urban Development has reported. Ingestion of lead-based paint chips can result in brain damage, so young children should be kept from them.

If your inspector finds relatively small areas of lead-based paint, the problem can be easily solved, either by scraping the paint and vacuuming the lead dust or by covering the painted surface with plastic. A large-scale lead-paint abatement job, though, may take weeks and cost $5,000–$10,000. Again, if the house you're buying is loaded with lead paint, either find another house or slash your offering price.

Avoid Interest-Rate Roulette

While you're shopping for a home, you'll probably be shopping for a mortgage, too. Speak with several prospective lenders, to see what terms they'll be willing to offer. Your first choice probably should be a *fixed-rate* mortgage, because you'll have level payments for the life of the loan; but sometimes *adjustable-rate* mortgages (ARMs) are attractive. If you choose an ARM, make sure there's a lifetime cap—a maximum rate that the lender can charge, no matter what happens to interest rates.

When mortgage rates are volatile, finding the right mortgage rate can be tricky. Will you pay the rate in effect at the time of your application, at the time of loan approval, or when the real-estate closing takes place? A difference of 0.5 percent or 0.75 percent can mean thousands of dollars, over the life of the mortgage.

You may be able to "lock in" a rate by paying a fee ranging from a few hundred dollars up to 1 percent of the loan amount. If you pay a large fee, make *sure* you're getting a win-win deal, in which case your mortgage rate can go *down*, if rates fall before the deal closes, but not *up*.

Security—at a Price

When you buy a house with a mortgage, you'll have to decide about mortgage insurance. That is, should you buy a policy that will pay off the mortgage if you die and continue making payments if you become disabled?

If your lender insists upon such coverage, there's little you can do but buy it. However, if you have the option, you're better off passing up this coverage. Instead, increase your *regular life* and *disability* insurance by enough to handle this obligation. You'll wind up paying much less.

For example: a thirty-year-old man might pay $350–$400 per year for $100,000 worth of mortgage insurance. That same home buyer likely can purchase $100,000 worth of *term life* insurance for under $200 in the first year. It's true that the gap will narrow as the home buyer grows older, but it will be many years before the term insurance is more expensive than mortgage insurance. By that time, the insured might have bought a new house.

Also, by buying the added life insurance, instead of mortgage insurance, this man gives his spouse an option. When she collects the life-insurance proceeds, she can decide whether to pay off the mortgage or continue the tax-deductible payments.

Similarly, disability insurance bought especially to pay off a lender is usually more expensive than ordinary disability coverage. The same reasoning holds for any type of credit insurance: You're better off increasing your basic coverage. That's true also for "gimmick" insurance, such as policies that will make mortgage payments in case you lose your job. Rather than buy overpriced policies, protect yourself by increasing your savings or establishing lines of credit.

Default Lines

Another type of mortgage insurance is *default* insurance: If you buy a house with a down payment of less than 10 percent, you'll likely have to buy an insurance policy that protects the lender if you don't make the mortgage payments. Such insurance is expensive, effectively adding 4 percent to 5 percent per year to a mortgage rate. Thus, a 7.5 percent mortgage becomes a 12 percent mortgage. To add insult to injury, the insurance premiums aren't deductible.

The *good* news is that the insurance can be dropped once your equity reaches 20 percent, generally because the value of the house has appreciated. However, lenders are not always required to *tell* you that the insurance can be dropped. It may be up to *you* to have the house appraised, so that you can stop paying the insurance premiums.

Say you buy a $100,000 house with a $10,000 down payment. You might have to pay an extra $350 up front, plus $300 per year for mortgage insurance. If your home increases in value to $110,000, then 80 percent of its value is $88,000. As long as your mortgage balance has fallen below $88,000, you have more than 20 percent equity. (That is, your mortgage debt is less than 80 percent of the home's value.) You can then stop paying mortgage insurance.

Your best strategy is to make a down payment of at least 20 percent, so you can avoid mortgage insurance in the first place. If at all possible, *don't* buy a house until you *have* a 20 percent down payment! (If that's *not* possible, then keep track of your home's appreciation, and have the place appraised once your equity goes over the 20 percent mark.)

Lemon Aid

You should exercise as much caution when buying a car as when buying a house, especially now that the kind of car you want may cost at least $20,000. Shop tough—take your time, compare features and prices, and discount baloney. If you're inclined to look for bargains, services such as AutoAdvisor (800-326-1976), Carbargains (800-475-7283), and Consumers Automotive (703-631-5161) claim to be able to deliver the car of your choice at *thousands* of dollars below sticker price, even *after* their fees are included. They assert, for example, that a $20,000 Ford Taurus would cost you around $16,250.

When you buy a *used* car, you need to exercise extra caution. Unless you're a first-rate mechanic, have a knowledgeable friend (or someone from your service station) check out a used car before you buy. Or pay $50–$100 to have someone from a franchised inspection service give the car a thorough going-over.

Should you finance a car purchase? Probably not, if you can avoid that. Why borrow at 8 percent (1994 rates) when you can't deduct the interest? You're better off paying cash, even if you have to pull money from a bank account paying 3 percent.

Increasingly, people are deciding not to buy their cars at all, but rather to *lease*. Leasing means a much smaller up-front outlay and smaller monthly payments. The problem is that all those payments don't *buy* you anything. If you're the type of person who isn't concerned about ownership but does want a late-model car every few years, leasing may just be for you. But if you're in the habit of keeping cars for six to ten years (or longer), buying is easily the better deal.

Lease at Leisure

Whether buying or leasing, beware of scam artists. Some unscrupulous auto dealers will "sell" a car to a consumer, then write up the contract as if it were a lease. The buyers wind up not owning the car. This fraud is often perpetrated on older consumers.

One elderly Florida couple fell victim to another scam. They wanted to lease, but they used a trade-in to knock down the price of the car to be leased from $20,000 to $18,000. The lease documents, however, were based on the $20,000 price. In effect, this elderly couple traded in their old car for nothing.

The way to protect yourself is to negotiate a price for a car, whether or not you intend to buy or lease. If you're going to lease, demand to see, in writing, the "capitalized cost" of the car, the price that's built into the lease.

Another approach is to first negotiate a lease without a trade-in. Then offer your old car and see how the monthly lease rate comes down. On a three-year lease, for example, a $7,000 trade-in should reduce your monthly payments by around $200 apiece. In any event, get more than one lease quote and take the time to read any contract carefully before signing.

Passwords to Privacy

Increasingly, computers are becoming part of our households. You certainly won't spend as much on a computer as on a house or car, but a computer's value goes well beyond the hardware alone. If you keep financial records on a computer, if you run your own business, or even if you're self-employed, it's vital that you protect your computer data. You don't want to lose them, and you certainly don't want anyone else to have access to them.

Unfortunately, there are many computer-wise thieves out there, and the number is sure to increase. To protect your hard disk, diskettes, and e-mail, you may want to use *encryption*. In essence, encryption is the process of taking your standard computer file and modifying it with a *key*, or *password*. Then your files and your transmissions can be read only by those to whom you entrust the key.

A number of programs are available that provide computer privacy, and more undoubtedly are on the way. (As of this writing, encryption programs were to some extent being held up by federal government demands for a standard system that the government will be able to access.) The following are some rules to keep in mind when choosing passwords—as well as access numbers to bank cash machines and long-distance phone services:

1. Don't use standard words. Some high-tech criminals run automated dictionary programs that test virtually every word in the language in which the document is written as a possible password.

2. Use a mix of letters, numbers, and oddball keyboard symbols—@, #, $, and so on.

3. Use long passwords (at least eight characters).

4. Don't use passwords that might be easy to guess, such as your initials, your home address, or your kids' birth dates.

5. Never write down your password and then leave it where some-

one might find it—especially near your computer. If you *must* write
it down, write it backwards, or begin with the third character, or find
some other method of camouflage.

6. Change passwords frequently.

7. Never tell anyone else your password, especially over the
phone—and never let anyone watch you enter it.

Computer Cautions

In addition to using passwords, some other basic precautions should
be followed. Use surge protecters (plug strips) to guard against sudden changes in the power supply known as "spikes." "Save" your work
frequently, and store copies on diskettes as well as on a hard drive.
Keep labeled diskettes in a secure storage case.

When you travel, carry your laptops, palmtops, etc., with you rather
than check them with your baggage. Use a padded case, preferably
one that's anonymous enough not to tell the world "A computer lives
here." Many portable computers come with security cables—which
should be used.

Your personal computer may not be covered by your standard
homeowners policy, especially if you use it for business. If that's the
case, you generally can buy specialized insurance to protect a PC from
fire, theft, accidents, and other hazards. The annual cost is usually
modest—$75 or less per year.

Card-Sharp

Whenever you're buying computers or other electronic items, home
furnishings, clothing, jewelry, and so on, use a credit card if possible.
You may find it a lot easier to straighten out subsequent problems if
you buy on your plastic.

In certain circumstances, the federal Fair Credit Billing Act protects you in cases of defective goods or services. Generally, your protection is greatest for charges over $50, especially if the sale took place
within 100 miles of your home address, or elsewhere in your home
state. You can withhold payment for goods or services in question,
offering instead a full explanation in writing. Now you have a heavy-
weight (the credit-card issuer) on your side as you try to seek satisfaction from the merchant. For a brochure on "Solving Your Credit
Card Billing Questions," send $1 to Bankcard Holders of America,
560 Herndon Parkway, Suite 120, Herndon, VA 22070.

SUMMING UP

• Not only should you shop thoroughly for a house, but also you should insist on an independent inspection before buying.

• If the inspection turns up major defects, you should find another house, drop your bid accordingly, or insist that the flaws be satisfactorily repaired before the sale.

• Fixed-rate mortgages usually make the best sense because you avoid the risk of sharply higher payments if rates rise.

• Credit life and credit disability insurance tend to be extremely expensive, so you're probably better off covering those risks by increasing your standard life and disability insurance.

• If you're buying a used car, have someone who's knowledgeable check it over carefully first.

• Auto leasing is increasingly popular, but scam artists are moving in, so you should take time to read any lease carefully before deciding whether to sign.

• Computer files and transmissions may contain valuable data, so you should protect them with backups and savvy password strategies.

• Whenever you make a big-ticket purchase, try to pay for it with a credit card, which may give you added leverage if a problem arises with the item.

Part III

Strictly Business

8

Inc. Spots

Trim Your Liability When You
Operate a Business

If you're a business owner, it's not hard to think up ways in which you can get wiped out by a huge award against you for damages, such as can be levied if, for example, a customer falls down in your parking lot, your store, or your office; the delivery person driving your van causes an accident; or the tomatoes you've sold cause an entire family to become seriously ill. The list could go on and on. Just one misstep, followed by an adverse court decision, and *all* of your personal assets could be lost.

Therefore, if you run a business, you should incorporate. In effect, you will form a new entity—let's say the ABC Corporation. The customer who falls down might sue ABC Corp. and possibly win a substantial award, but your *personal* assets might be protected—perhaps even fully.

But corporate status isn't an *absolute* barrier against claims. In some cases, courts have been willing to "pierce the corporate veil," allowing suits to proceed against a corporation's owners—especially if their own negligence led to the problem. Moreover, many lenders require a *personal* guarantee on loans to small companies, so you're effectively putting your own assets behind corporate debt. Nevertheless, you have considerably more protection with a corporation than you have without it.

Real Time

Incorporating your business isn't difficult. Most lawyers will handle the paperwork for a modest fee of perhaps a few hundred dollars. However, if you want to enjoy all the protection that incorporation can provide, you have to observe all the formalities—your corporation must be a real one.

The document you receive when you incorporate, the *certificate of incorporation* (or *articles of incorporation*) should be reviewed regularly. If any information is not up-to-date, the certificate should be amended.

Many states permit corporations to indeminify their officers and directors from certain lawsuits. If your corporation's certificate does *not* include such a provision, you may wish to add one. Martin M. Shenkman, an attorney in Teaneck, New Jersey, provides the following example:

> The directors and officers of the Corporation shall be indemnified by the Corporation, to the maximum extent permitted under state law, against reasonable costs, expenses, and counsel fees paid or incurred in connection with any action, suit, or proceeding in which the director or officer or the legal representative of the director or officer is a party by reason of being or having been a director or officer of the Corporation. This indemnification shall be subject to any conditions, limitations, and restrictions as may be imposed by law and shall be, in addition to, and not in restriction or limitation of, any other privilege which the Corporation may otherwise have with respect to the indemnification or reimbursement of officers.

Up to the Minutes

Corporations should meet at least once a year to elect officers and directors, adopt certain agreements, and approve important contracts.

Formal minutes should be kept. In addition, you should keep complete books and records, have a separate corporate bank account, and file corporate tax returns. You'll thus be able to show that the corporation either does or did exist as a legal entity, and enjoy the benefits of limited shareholder liability.

However, just because you've incorporated, don't neglect simple prudence. You should carry business liability insurance, and adopt policies (e.g., shovel snow in the parking lot, check driving records of employees who operate company vehicles) to reduce the risk of accidents. Such precautions will help bolster your case if a mishap occurs and a lawsuit is brought.

Two Paths to Protection

When you decide to incorporate, you also have to decide which type of corporation to use:

• *C corporation.* This is a regular corporation, subject to a corporate income tax. Thus, profits probably will be taxed twice—at the corporate level, and again on your personal return—when you take the money out. Also, C corporation losses can't be deducted on your personal return.

C corporations have other advantages. Health insurance, as well as some other fringe benefits, can prove deductible. Lenders often prefer dealing with C corporations because this is the traditional form. Plus, C corporations offer considerable flexibility when you want to pass them on to family members or employees. In general, if you expect to pay out virtually all of your earnings as compensation to employees (including yourself), you can operate a C company and *not* have to pay corporate income tax—because the company will have little or no income.

• *S corporation.* This is the alternative corporate form. You can elect S corporation status if your company meets certain criteria, such as having no more than thirty-five shareholders and only one class of stock.

If you qualify, S corporations can be great tax shelters because they're exempt from the corporate income tax. All corporate earnings are taxed on your personal tax return. If the company operates at a loss, that loss likely can be deducted on your personal tax return.

S corporations offer relief from many other tax headaches that plague C corporations, including the unreasonable compensation tax, the excess accumulated earnings tax, the personal holding company tax, and the corporate alternative minimum tax. On the other hand, fringe benefits aren't deductible if they're enjoyed by the primary shareholders, and the restrictions on ownership may interfere with estate planning. So check with a tax pro before electing S status.

For S corporations as well as C corporations, shareholders enjoy *limited* liability.

Staying Within the Limits

Besides incorporating, there are two other ways to run a business and still limit your liability for business-related claims:

• *Limited partnership.* In most partnerships, all partners are liable for all obligations of the partnership. Several law and accounting firms have felt the pinch in recent years, when hit by large awards for damages.

Limited partnerships, on the other hand, have two classes of partners: *limited* and *general.* Whereas general partners share full liability, limited partners' liability is limited to the cash they contribute and notes they sign. In some cases the general partner may be a corporation with limited liability, while most of the money flows to limited partners who also enjoy protection.

Often the limited partnership structure is used for investment real estate and other types of ventures wherein passive investors don't want to incur the risks of running a business.

• *Limited liability company (LLC).* This is a relatively new vehicle, but it's rapidly gaining popularity: In 1994, over half the states recognized LLCs, with more certain to join in.

In essence, an LLC is a cross between an S corporation and a partnership. Just as in the case of an S corporation, LLC owners enjoy limited liability. Again, there is no corporate income tax, so all income or loss is passed through to the owners' personal tax returns.

However, LLCs are not subject to the same restrictions as S corporations. For example, there is no limit to the number or type of owners, the latter of which might include trusts or corporations. Too, profits and losses can be divided disproportionately, if desired, which isn't so for an S corporation.

If your state recognizes the LLC, consider adopting it for your business. You can get limited liability, tax benefits, and flexibility. As

LLCs become more widely accepted, they likely will become the standard structure for small businesses.

Exit Laughing

If you're a co-owner of a business or investment venture, you should always have an up-to-date buy–sell agreement, no matter what type of business structure you use. A buy–sell agreement protects you and your family in case of retirement, death, or disability. If you don't have one, or if it's obsolete, the result can be disastrous.

Take the case of Wally W., who formed a partnership back in 1968 with Jack J. They bought investment property in Manhattan for $150,000 and signed a buy–sell. If one partner died, the survivor would buy the decedent's share for $75,000. After eighteen years of a real-estate boom, Wally died and Jack bought Wally's half of the property from Wally's estate for $75,000. Then he turned around and sold the building for over $1.6 million!

Wally's estate sued, but the New York County Surrogate Court upheld the transaction. The old buy–sell, which never had been updated, was ruled still valid. Wally's heirs got $75,000 instead of $800,000. So be sure your buy–sell agreement is revised regularly.

SUMMING UP

- Small-business owners are vulnerable to financially crippling lawsuits resulting from accidents or other causes.
- Incorporating your business doesn't give you absolute protection, but it can help, particularly in cases where you haven't been personally negligent.
- Even if you incorporate, you should carry business liability insurance and take precautions to avoid disasters.
- To enjoy limited liability from incorporating, your corporation should be a real one, complying with all the paperwork requirements.
- Corporations should hold meetings at least once a year, and formal minutes should be kept.
- Regular C corporations permit you to deduct fringe benefits, but they're subject to the corporate income tax.
- S corporations offer many tax advantages, including exemption

from the corporate income tax, but there are strict requirements for S status.

• Limited partnerships can be structured so that passive investors are limited partners, without exposure to partnership liability.

• Limited liability corporations, new vehicles that offer the best features of S corporations and partnerships, may become the preferred form of small-business ownership.

9

Territorial Imperative

Salespeople, Protect Your Livelihood

Plastic comes, software goes. There's always some "sure" sector of the economy that's bound to prosper in the coming years, an industry in which men and women can build secure careers. Then, after young strivers have become middle-aged middle managers, the bottom falls out and the companies cut back, assigning a lot of hard-to-employ white-collar workers to the jobless statistics columns.

There is one line of work where this isn't likely to occur, however— a profession most people can enter without going through years of medical or law school (or any other). You can *sell*. If you like to work with people and you're willing to put in long hours, you *can* succeed as a salesperson. In today's lingo, you'll become a "producer," bringing in business. As long as you produce, there will always be a way for you to earn a living, either as an employee or as an independent contractor.

For salespeople, the biggest threat is the loss of a *territory*—in this case perhaps a geographical region, an industry, or any grouping of customers. If your employer or principal takes away the customer base you've helped to build, you've lost your greatest asset.

How can you protect yourself? Demand a contract up front. Naturally, if you're an independent rep, you'll want a contract with each principal, spelling out the terms of each relationship. And salespeople who are employees should have contracts, too. Yours may not be easy to get when you're starting out, but after you've become a producer and employers are vying for your services, you should be able to negotiate a formal contract.

Sellers Keepers

The most important point in a sales contract is your ability to keep your customers after the contract terminates. If the contract says that the customers belong to the company, you can be in trouble. In sales, prospecting is 90 percent of the effort; you go to a lot of trouble to find customers and convince them to rely on you. If you can't take your clients with you, no matter where you go, your prior efforts will be wasted.

Some contracts do in fact contain what's known as a *noncompete clause* stating that after you break off a relationship, you won't be able to work in the same field as your former employer—generally for a specified time period. Such clauses may amount to restraint of trade, and if they do, they can be overturned in court. Nevertheless, you want to avoid costly litigation, if possible. So beware of such provisions when considering signing a contract.

Of course, you may think you're perfectly happy with your employer, and that your employer is happy with you, so why bother with a contract? However, few people—especially salespeople—stay with one employer during their entire career. At some point, a parting of the ways is likely. You'll be in a much better position if you have a formal contract, and especially one that a knowledgeable lawyer has looked over (*not* overlooked) before advising you to sign.

Loyalty Test

Aside from a formal contract, the key to self-preservation for salespeople is having a loyal customer base. Your customers *must* trust you and believe in your integrity. Those benefits being the case, if you move from one company to another your customers will find a way to move with you. But if you're just an order taker, your customers won't make the slightest effort to stay with you.

You must in effect bind your customers to you. You want them to have confidence in you, to be comfortable with you. The best way to accomplish this is to listen to what your customers have to say—really *listen*. They'll tell you, in one way or another, what they want and what they need. And if you supply what they ask for, they'll be *your* customers, not your company's.

Beyond this basic exercise in salesmanship, people appreciate thoughtfulness. When you meet with a new client, ask for some personal information—name, address, family members, dates of birth. Then, make it a point to send birthday cards each year. You might want to add an inexpensive gift: an inspirational book, a pen, a pocket calculator. Everybody likes to be remembered, and everybody likes to receive gifts (as long as it's clear that no bribe is intended).

While you're making an effort to think about your customers, think about your support staff, too—whether they're your employees, or coworkers. Their cooperation can make a world of difference to your professional success. For example, suppose you know that one of your support people has been working hard and is going to take a break by going out to dinner with his or her spouse. If you can, find out which restaurant they'll be dining at, call the place, and ask to have the meal charged to your credit card. Your efforts will be greatly appreciated and, for a fairly modest amount, you'll earn the loyalty of colleagues as well as customers.

Fireproof

Whether or not you're in sales, you have a "territory" to protect. That territory might be your job, your rung on the corporate ladder, or your niche in a sideline business. If someone else takes over that territory, your future income is in trouble. So take some basic steps to protect your livelihood. Keep learning new skills, and new applications for your existing ones. Find out what your particular strengths are (you're a whiz at soothing ruffled customers, for example), and focus on those areas.

No matter how safe or happy you are at your current position, don't be complacent. The job that you hold for forty years, from school until retirement, just about doesn't exist anymore. Conditions change, managements change, and you could find yourself on the wrong end of a "restructuring." So keep your eyes and ears open at all times. Attend industry meetings and make your presence known. Swap business cards. Find out who's expanding and where the job opportunities are likely to be. And keep your options open.

Now here's the one to memorize right away: At the first sign that your employer might be in trouble (the first rumor, even), start networking in earnest, looking for a more secure position.

The situation you want to avoid, if possible, is one in which your income depends on one person's good graces. No matter how well you get along with your boss, and how terrific he or she seems to be, don't hitch your wagon to just that star. Your boss might get sick, get fired, or have a change of heart. *Always* have a fallback position—at least instantly in mind.

The same principle applies if you have your own company or a sideline business: Don't focus all of your efforts on *one* customer. That one might find another supplier or, even worse, stick you with a large pile of unpaid receivables.

If you *must* rely on just one customer (or even a few of them), protect yourself by hedging your risks. One way to reduce your exposure is to work with an experienced *factor* (broker, money lender, etc.) who might advance you 70 percent to 75 percent of the face value of your invoice as soon as they're generated, with the balance sent to you when the bill is paid. Besides minimizing your exposure to bad debts, factors can provide you with immediate working capital, enabling you to expand your business.

Factors may also check the credit of prospects before they become customers, then accept invoices from approved accounts. This type of factoring is often done on a "nonrecourse" basis: You have *no* credit risk, even if the customer defaults. In effect, a factor can act as your credit *and* collection department, freeing you up to spend full time building your business.

SUMMING UP

• Although successful salespeople can make money in all economic circumstances, they need to diligently protect their customer base.

• You should have a contract that permits you to take your customers with you, upon your termination, with no restrictions on your future ability to compete against your present employer.

• The more customer loyalty you can build, the more likely you'll keep those customers as you move from job to job.

• You should make every effort to be on good terms with your support people, who can provide considerable help to your career.

• No matter what you do for a living, you need to cultivate other people, inside and outside of your company, so you'll have easier access to a new job in case you're laid off.

• Never put your future in the hands of one person or one company (other than yourself, of course).

• Hedge your risks by developing skills that are in wide demand, and by serving a variety of customers.

10

Wine 'Em and Dine 'Em

Get a Payoff From Your Business Entertainment Dollars

In some businesses you have to entertain: Clients expect to be taken out to lunch, to dinner, to sports events. If you don't entertain them, your competitors will. Effective entertaining is absolutely necessary to protect your business interests. However, effective entertaining is more than just spending money on customers and prospects. You have to make sure you get *value* for your money.

If most of your business entertainment takes place in one area—near your home or your office—you should focus on only one or two restaurants. Be a galloping gourmet on your own time. When it comes to business entertaining, be strictly business.

Pick restaurants that make sense for your industry. If you're in fashions, for example, or in advertising, you probably will want to select a trendy spot where people go to see and be seen.

In most businesses that's not the case. You should choose restaurants with a basic American menu from which virtually every client can choose something good to eat. Also, there should be ample (but not overpowering) lighting, so you can take notes if need be. Tables should be far apart, and the noise level should be low, so you and your clients can talk business without hearing everyone else's business.

Once you have found one or two places that meet these criteria, go back again and again. You'll know what you're getting, with no surprises (which often turn out to be unpleasant). The restaurant's management will get to know you well, and value you all the more as a customer. You'll be given good tables, and personalized service that will impress your clients.

No Check, Please

You can establish a private line of credit with such restaurants, or give them your credit card number. Leave instructions that all of your meals be charged to that account, along with a 20 percent service fee. No bill need be brought to the table. Thus, you'll avoid awkward sparring with clients as to who picks up the check.

Spread a little money around—it doesn't have to be a lot. Give a $20 bill to the owner or maître d', or to the chef. Your clients certainly will be impressed when you're greeted by name at the door, or when the chef comes out of the kitchen to say hello.

Pay attention to the doorman, too, when you're at a hotel or another establishment that employs such a person. Give him $10 to "watch" your car for you, and it likely will be sitting there waiting for you when you come out (whereas many other patrons will have to wait for valet parking to get theirs).

If you *must* use valet parking, be careful to turn over your ignition key, and no others. You don't want someone else having access to your trunk, where you might keep samples, papers, and other valuables. And you certainly don't want to put your house keys in the hands of a stranger.

Beyond maître d's, chefs, and doormen, be reasonably generous with waiters, waitresses, and bartenders: Tip 20 percent rather than 15 percent of the bill. The extra money isn't great ($2 on a $40 meal), and the goodwill you'll earn will be considerable. No salesperson should *ever* be known as a poor tipper.

Note-Worthy

There's one more step you need to take to get the most from your business entertainment dollars: Keep thorough records. If you *do*, you can deduct those bucks. (Actually, you can deduct 50 percent of them, under the 1993 tax law.) If you *don't* have records, you're apt to find yourself entertaining an IRS auditor.

The tax laws in this area are complicated, but entertaining is deductible if you make a genuine effort either to get new business or to maintain business you already have. There should be a reasonable prospect of a profitable return, too. If you take someone to a $100 dinner for the chance to make a one-time sale of $10 worth of housewares, the IRS might reject your deduction on the ground that it wasn't "ordinary and necessary." (You don't have to land a big deal in order to write off a meal, but you do at least need to make a real effort to obtain *some* amount of lucrative business.)

A daily diary or pocket notebook can substantiate your deductions. Just write down all the details—whom you entertained, where, how much you spent. Add a few words about the business purpose of the meal, and what you discussed. If you pay with a credit card, fasten your receipt to that page in the diary. Your accountant will appreciate your diligence, the IRS will focus its attention instead on taxpayers who try to re-create expenses, and you'll get the tax deductions to which you're entitled.

SUMMING UP

• If business entertaining is vital to your career, you should make the most of the money you spend.

• Limit yourself to one or two good restaurants as settings for most of your entertaining.

• At your regular business-meal restaurants, tip a little bit extra—and spread some money around—so you'll get personalized service whenever you entertain there.

• By keeping careful records, you'll be able to deduct 50 percent of your bona fide business entertainment costs.

Part IV

Foreign Affairs

11

Travel Smart

Keep Your Guard Up While You're on the Road

Vacations should be carefree but not careless. There are virtually no safe havens today, either in the United States or abroad. Wherever you go, you need to protect your property—not to mention your life. That's true whether you're on a solo business trip or a family holiday.

What can go wrong? Let us count the ways:

• *You could lose your luggage.* U.S. airlines report over two million instances of lost, damaged, or stolen baggage per year. Even if you get your luggage back, your trip could be ruined.

• *Your rental car could be stolen—or worse.* Florida, in particular, has experienced horrendous instances of carjackings and tourist murders.

• *You can be robbed or assaulted in your hotel.* Year after year, over 10,000 lawsuits are filed against U.S. hotels for negligent security.

• *Your credit cards might be stolen.* Hundreds of millions of dollars are lost each year to fraudulent use of credit cards. If you're ripped off, your own losses might be limited, but you'll suffer considerable aggravation and loss of time.

• *Your passport could be stolen.* Over 10,000 Americans reported passport theft during 1993.

• *Your telephone bill could skyrocket.* When you make a phone call from a hotel lobby or an airport, using your long-distance card, make sure no one else can see the buttons you push, or hear the number you give the operator. Thieves have been known to use telephoto lenses and mirrors as spy devices. If you can, use a phone with an electronic eye, permitting you to slide your card past it to get a reading.

In other words, never let your guard down. No matter if you're traveling on the world's finest airline, staying at a luxury hotel, or eating at a gourmet restaurant, you need to be constantly on your guard.

Too Good to Be True

Travel fraud starts even before you do. You might, for example, get a letter or a phone call announcing that you've won a "free trip," or a special packaged deal. All you need to do is give the "travel agent" your credit card number and expiration date.

Naturally, there isn't any free or bargain trip. You'll never receive the promised tickets. You *will* receive, though, credit card statements showing large charges for items you never purchased or ordered. (In a variation on this scheme you'll be asked to make a deposit—which you'll never get back.)

Don't fall for these illusory deals. *No one* is going to send you to Hawaii for $100. *Don't* give your credit card information to strangers! Instead, deal only with reputable travel agents. Book your trip through someone you know personally, or with an agent who has been recommended to you. The first time around, you might want to visit the agent in person, so you can size up the operation. No agent will be able to get you free trips, but a reliable one will have access to a computer system that can find the best available values for you.

Now You See Them . . .

Pay for travel with a credit card. Herta F., of New York City, wishes she had. Herta booked a tour of Southeast Asia and sent a certified check for $5,900 to her travel agency. The money never was forwarded to the airline and, by the time Herta discovered the omission, her travel agent was in bankruptcy, with $2 million in debts and $20,000 in assets. Herta didn't even bother to sue. If she had paid for the tour with a credit card, she might have been able to refuse to pay the charge, or even receive a refund from the card issuer.

Gail M., of Piscataway, New Jersey, had somewhat better luck when she lost $10,000 on a tour to Egypt in 1989, after the tour operator collapsed. She sued her travel agent and got back around $2,000, which the agent had received as a commission. She also was able to get back the $2,000 deposit she had put on her American Express card, although it took a year-long struggle. She was out the rest of the money, which she had paid by check—but at least it wasn't a total loss.

When a retiree like Herta or a secretary like Gail loses $6,000, that can be a heartbreaking disaster. Multiply them by the thousands and you get the $12 billion that consumers lose each year on busted tours, according to the National Consumers League.

So, how can *you* avoid being victimized? You should always pay with a credit card if your tour operator or travel agent will accept one. As mentioned, the federal Fair Credit Billing Act gives you sixty days from the date of the bill to contest a charge. For trips, MasterCard extends the deadline to 120 days, while Visa allows 120 days from the date of travel. American Express is even more flexible, sometimes allowing you a year to dispute payment. Sometimes a credit card issuer will even provide travel insurance if you pay with its card.

Whether or not you pay by credit card, however, check on the tour operator before paying. Call the airline or the main hotel you'll be using, and find out if the tour operator has lived up to its promises on previous trips. Call the U.S. Tour Operators Association (USTOA) (212-750-7371) and the National Tour Association (NTA) (800-682-8886) to find out if the operator is a current member in good standing. If so, there will be a guarantee fund you can tap in case a member tour operator fails; the USTOA guarantee generally is stronger.

Risky Business

There are many types of specialized travel insurance you can buy before you go. On the whole, you should save your money. For example, some airlines will sell you additional baggage insurance, but such coverage is expensive and loaded with exclusions—buy it only if your luggage contains something of great value. You're much better off not packing real valuables in baggage that you'll check with the airline.

Don't buy life or dismemberment insurance from an airport vending machine, the kind that pays off only in a plane crash. (In Part V of this book, we'll show you how to buy the right kind of health, life, and disability insurance. If those are all in place, you don't need special accident insurance.)

Trip-cancellation insurance has its place, but it isn't for everyone. If you have to cancel because a previously existing medical condition flares up, the policy may not pay. You won't have this problem if you buy a refundable ticket, or one in exchange for which the airline will reissue a ticket for a different date, charging you only a modest fee.

However, if you get a fabulous deal on a nonrefundable ticket, you might *want* to put some of your savings into trip-cancellation and interruption insurance. When Hugo M., a New Jersey retiree, had to miss a vacation in New Orleans because of an unexpected heart-by-pass operation, he and his wife got back $2,400 from Travel Guard International. Such insurance (sold by most travel agents) typically costs $5.50 per $100 of coverage. Thus, it would cost about $135 to protect a $2,400 trip. Besides personal illnesses, such insurance should entitle you to a refund under other circumstances, such as the death of a family member.

Trip-cancellation insurance may protect you if a tour operator goes out of business, but some policies provide coverage only if the operator files for bankruptcy protection—which isn't always the case. If you're going on a packaged tour and you're considering trip-cancellation insurance, buy only if you'll be reimbursed for *all* tour operator failures. The trip-cancellation offered by American Express (800-234-0375), Access America (800-284-8300), and Travel Guard International (800-826-1300) is stronger than the insurance sold by tour operators, which would be worthless in case of a business failure.

If you're going on a cruise, be wary of "cancellation waivers" offered by some cruise lines. These waivers, which cost $60–$80, allow you to escape cancellation penalties if an accident or illness occurs. However, some of these waivers *won't* protect you if you cancel within seventy-two hours of departure time. Try to find a waiver that lets you cancel closer to sailing time.

Leave Home Without It

You don't need to take all your credit cards when you travel. Leave any *local* cards at home. Generally, all you'll need is an American Express card, and either a Visa or a MasterCard, plus an ATM card and a telephone calling card. If you have AT&T's Universal Card, for example, it serves not only as a Visa or MasterCard but also as a phone card and an ATM access card.

Just as you should leave some of your credit cards at home when you're going on a business or pleasure trip, you also should leave your car at home, in a locked garage, and take a cab. Taking your own car and leaving it in a long-term parking lot is like putting a "take me" sign on the windshield. If your car isn't stolen, it could easily be vandalized by thieves breaking in to steal parts.

For instance: Your car's internal computer (the device that controls the fuel-injection system and other functions) is highly prized. It has no vehicle ID number on it, can be resold for hundreds of dollars, and is quickly removed through the dashboard or glove compartment. Once someone takes your electronic module, your car can't operate—so you'll need to have it towed to a repair shop.

Few long-term parking lots have the security necessary to thwart thieves. If you absolutely *must* leave your car in a long-term lot, park under a light, as near as possible to the booth where operators collect parking fees. Never leave *anything* of value in the car. And be especially wary when walking to and from your car—particularly after dark.

SUMMING UP

• Crime against travelers is widespread, so you must be vigilant whenever you're away from home.

• Book all trips through reputable travel agents rather than falling for telephone come-ons, and pay with a credit card if you can.

• To protect yourself against tour cancellations, check out the tour operator carefully.

• If you decide you need trip-cancellation insurance, buy from an established third party instead of from a tour operator.

• You generally should skip other types of specialized travel insurance, relying instead on standard health, life, disability, and home-owners insurance.

- When you travel, take only a few, necessary credit cards.
- Leave your car at home rather than expose it to thieves in an airport long-term parking lot.

12

An Ounce of Prevention

Property Protection Shouldn't
Stop at Home

Many travelers view airports and hotels as sanctuaries. Everyone there is just like you—prosperous people determined to enhance their success on a business trip, or enjoy a needed respite while on vacation. There's no need to feel threatened.

Don't fall into that trap! Just as Willie Sutton robbed banks because that's where the money was, today's thieves go where the best pickings are: relaxed, guards-down travelers laden with cash, travelers checks, jewelry, cameras, and expensive clothes. Airports and hotels teem with predators—so you need to keep constantly vigilant to avoid becoming their prey.

Baggage Handling

For short trips, travel as lightly as you can, and carry your luggage onto the plane with you. Stow it in an overhead compartment or in the area allotted for hanging bags. That way, you'll *know* your bag will arrive with you. You'll save time, too, on arrival at your destination.

If you *must* check your luggage, make sure each piece is secured— perhaps even with a small padlock. To thwart thieves who may have keys that fit a variety of luggage or key-operated locks, use a *combination* lock.

Never put your home address on your baggage tag, because a sharp- eyed thief can spot your address and go immediately to your empty house, probably free to take whatever is in there. Instead, put your *office* address on the tag. Before each trip, also put your destination phone number on the tag, so you can be reached in case your bag goes astray—innocently or otherwise.

Put something distinctive on each piece of luggage, too—colored tape or yarn around the handles, for example—so no one takes your bags by mistake. Colorful luggage straps are widely available. Sam- sonite makes beige or gray luggage straps that even include built-in combination locks.

Partners in Crime

Not only may your luggage be sent to the wrong place by accident, but also, dishonest airline employees are capable of stealing it from under everyone else's nose. Sometimes a ticketing agent or curbside baggage handler will be working with a confederate who loads the planes. If you look particularly prosperous, or if there's some indi- cation that your bags could be holding valuables, the baggage check- in people might mark them with a distinctive "tipoff" coding so they'll be separated out, and never reach the plane. Or, your bags may be intentionally misrouted to an airport where an accomplice will be waiting with itchy palms.

So don't do anything to draw attention to either yourself or your baggage. Dress down when you travel, and don't flash expensive jew- elry. Your best bet is to buy midpriced rather than top-of-the-line luggage. Just to be on the safe side, don't put valuables in your lug- gage, either: Keep all cash, jewelry, cameras, and vital papers with *you* when you travel. (If you read your airline ticket closely, you'll learn that the carrier bears no responsibility for lost jewelry, furs, antiques, and electronic equipment.)

Whenever you have any problem with your luggage, act right away. If you don't file a claim *within four hours* of your flight's arrival, most airlines won't recognize *any* responsibility. And even within that time period, airlines are picky about what they'll pay—you're in a stronger position if you can prove what was in your baggage, generally with receipts. So, if you're returning from a trip on which you've done a great deal of shopping, keep your receipts *with* you, rather than in your checked baggage.

Road Warriors

For many people, the first stop after arriving at their destination is the airport car-rental lot. You need to get around, on a vacation or business trip, and that usually includes having to rent a car.

However, even the most casual watcher of TV news knows that carjacking has become a real scourge, and that airport car rentals are particularly vulnerable. Miami's airport may be the most notorious, but it's by no means the only danger spot for tourists. So be extra-cautious when you're renting a car!

If possible, avoid the airport car-rental scene altogether. When you make your travel plans, have your agent arrange for you to pick up a car at your hotel, or at a nearby rental outlet. Use a cab, or the hotel shuttle, to get both from and to the airport.

If you *must* rent at an airport, try to get there before dark. Your unfamiliarity with an area is accentuated, and thus your vulnerability is increased at night. Whichever way you handle the car-rental arrangement, always put your luggage in the trunk, not in the backseat—where the pieces are visible, like a beacon to thieves and carjackers.

Know Before You Go

Get your route down pat *before* you drive out of any car-rental lot. If you pull over to look at a map for directions, you might well be putting on a sheep costume in front of a lot of hungry wolves.

If you absolutely must ask for directions, be selective about whom you talk to. Your first choice should be someone in a uniform—police officer, mail carrier, utility worker. Those types probably will give you the best instructions, as well as not endanger you.

When you're riding on local streets, lock your doors and windows. If it's hot, run the air-conditioning and keep the car buttoned up. At stop lights, be ready for anything (including peeling rubber). If you feel threatened, hit the accelerator if that's at all possible—you can worry later about a ticket for running a light, or whatever.

Most of all, don't get out of your car if you have any doubts *at all* about your circumstances. A favorite trick of carjackers is to bump you enough to cause a minor accident, so you'll pull over. When you do, and get out of the car to check insurance cards, you'll find yourself looking straight into a barrelful of lead poison. Not only your car, but also your luggage and your personal possessions, will disappear— probably forever. Some carjackers even shoot first and take later.

If you're in a fender-bender, don't pull over right away. Drive slowly to a well-lit area, with lots of traffic, before getting out of your car. If you don't like the looks of the people in the other vehicle, just keep going until you reach your hotel or other destination.

Similarly, don't stop for hitchhikers or people in distress, no matter how forlorn or attractive. Don't take a chance that the helpless-looking soul on the highway isn't a decoy for well-armed pals. If you really want to help a stranded motorist, note the location and call the police later, from a safe locale.

A common variation on the entrapment theme is the one in which a pedestrian jumps what looks to be in front of your car, and then falls down, as if injured. If this happens, *stay in your car*. Otherwise, when you get out to check, you might be walking right into an armed robbery—your own.

No Room for Carelessness

Even when you arrive at your hotel, you're *still* not home free. Hotels are riskier places than you think—especially big-city convention hotels. Almost anybody can wander in and out, at any time—there are no security checks or metal detectors at the doors.

Don't use your official title when making reservations. But *do* ask for a room between the second and seventh floors; that will give you some protection from ground-level, walk-in thieves but still leave you low enough to evacuate easily in case of a fire or other emergency.

If you're staying at a bustling, large hotel, keep a wary eye on your bags when you check in. While you're worrying about your reservation, some sneak thief could be making off with your camera. The same caution is necessary when you check out and you're concentrating on your bill.

Better yet, choose a small hotel when you make your plans. Such hotels don't attract as many thieves, because people who don't belong there are more conspicuous.

When you check in, make sure the clerk doesn't blurt out your name and room number within earshot of a listener. If he or she does, whisper that you'd like a different room. *Never* give *anyone* you don't know your room number!

As for your room: Insist on at least double deadbolts and a peep-hole. (Coded electronic locks are even safer.) Those little chain locks won't stop a serious intruder.

Don't let into your room anyone you're not expecting. If someone says he or she is bringing you a gift of fruit or flowers from the management, call the front desk to confirm. It's better to feel a little foolish than to be victimized a lot.

Keep any valuables in a hotel's safe-deposit box, rather than leave them in your room. However, don't assume that even the box is burglarproof: If you store valuables in one, get an itemized receipt.

Trouble Spots

Whenever you can when you travel, keep bag and camera straps under your clothing, where they can't be grabbed. If someone does get a hand on your belongings, don't start a tug-of-war unless you're sure you'll win. Thieves don't think anything of dragging a victim into traffic, if necessary. In fact, you're better off without any kind of bag, keeping valuables in a zippered pouch you can wrap around your arm, leg, or waist.

Yes, the scams you see on TV really happen, so don't be fooled. If someone spills ketchup or mustard or taco sauce on you, secure your wallet or purse, and other money, in your pockets before worrying about the stain.

And don't fall for this one: You're walking along with your family, a camera around your neck loudly proclaiming your tourist status. Some nice-seeming guy offers to take a picture, using your camera. He backs up and backs up, to get a better shot, and—he's gone, without even asking you to say "cheese."

In some locations you need to be *extra* cautious. Here are some of the real danger zones, according to *Money* magazine:

• *New York City.* You might think you're relatively safe in midtown, but that's not always the case, especially on Fifth in the 50s, from Rockefeller Center to Trump Tower. A lot of pickpockets are around. Be wary of distractions, from loud arguments to jostling.

If you find yourself on the subway or bus, don't fall for the pickpocket scam: An accomplice hollers, "There's a pickpocket on this train [or bus]." Hearing this, the passengers all reach for their money, to see if it's still there. This shows the pickpocket, sitting where he can observe the passengers, exactly where to go to get the dough.

• *Los Angeles.* Be careful when you go to the beach. Thieves will smash your car windows and take anything they can from inside.

• *Miami.* Carjackers are always coming up with new tricks. Now they pull up alongside your car and yell "Fire." *Don't* pull over and get out of your car.

• *Las Vegas.* Women should watch their handbags, no matter how exciting the action in the casinos. One favorite thieves' ploy is to drop a few coins near a woman who has put her purse on a table or chair. When she reaches to help pick up the coins, her purse disappears.

SUMMING UP

• At every stage of your travels, vigilance is vital.

• Never put your home address on a luggage tag—instead, use your business address, and include the phone number at your destination.

• Don't pack valuables in checked baggage, and don't look conspicuously affluent while you travel.

• Try to avoid renting a car at an airport counter, especially after dark.

• Don't do anything to indicate you're a tourist, while in a rental car, and don't get out of the car unless you're in a well-traveled, well-lit area.

• In a hotel, watch your valuables at all times, and never let into your room anyone you're not expecting.

• While out sightseeing, be alert for scam artists who'll distract you and then rob you.

13

At Sea, Overseas

Coping With Foreign Catastrophes

The list of dangerous vacation destinations doesn't stop with New York, Los Angeles, Miami, and Las Vegas. Foreign thugs are just as eager to relieve you of your possessions as are their domestic counterparts. Here are a few places where you *must* travel with care:

• *Cancun, Mexico.* Beware of violent street thieves.

• *Kingston, Jamaica.* If you're offered a great deal on currency exchange, walk away: The money may be illegal. Stick with banks and authorized exchange offices. Similarly, if a youngster offers to show you around, for a low price, don't go along; related robberies and assaults have been reported. Pickpockets operate freely in the main streets of Jamaica's cities.

• *Europe.* Keep copies of all credit card transactions—small shops often add zeros to increase the amount.

One trouble spot for street crime is Paris, especially near the American Embassy and the American Express office. Gangs of kids waving newspapers will rip you off after you've been distracted.

- *Hong Kong.* Here's another place where credit card fraud is common, so keep your charge slips. Some merchants will sell you one thing, then put a cheap substitute in your parcel. Pickpockets are a problem here, too.
- *Egypt.* Reportedly, tourists have been targeted by Islamic radicals.
- *Rio de Janeiro.* Ipanema and Copacabana beaches have become infested with muggers, especially around twilight. If you must go surfward, make sure you're in a large group.
- *Moscow.* Dress inconspicuously, and travel in pairs everywhere. Even cab drivers will rob you! Also, don't see local doctors if you can possibly avoid doing so, because many are not up to western standards.
- *Nigeria.* As of this writing, the only airport in the world where the U.S. government explicitly warns of security risks is in Lagos, the capital. If you *must* go, fly on American Trans Air, which provides its own security to help protect passengers.

In 1994, the International Airline Passengers Association issued a list of dangerous destinations: China, South Korea, India, Central Africa, the former Soviet Union, Colombia, and the Andes region of South America. If you *must* fly to these areas, use only the best-known, safest airlines—generally, U.S. airlines or foreign national carriers.

China, for example, was reported to lack the infrastructure and trained personnel to handle that country's air traffic, as well as to have the worst air piracy record in the world. Similarly, air travel in central Africa is marred by hijackings, unsafe airports, and poor air-traffic control systems, the association reported.

For an updated report on high-crime areas, call the State Department at 202-647-5225; the modem number is 202-647-9225. In general, for security as well as safety reasons, you're better off flying on a heavily regulated American airline (although some foreign carriers, such as Israel's El Al, are comfortingly vigilant about security).

By the Numbers

When you're traveling outside the United States, someone at home should have the numbers of both your passport and your traveler's checks, as well as a list of the credit cards you take with you, along with phone numbers usable to report lost or stolen cards. If you don't want to impose on a friend or relative, your credit card issuer may offer automatic cancellation service (generally costing $20–$30 per year).

Foreign travelers should take additional phone numbers with them. Wherever you go, *make sure* you have the number of the local U.S. Embassy, Consul, or regional security offices, as well as the twenty-four-hour number of the U.S. Mission. You can get these numbers from the State Department (202-647-4000) before you leave.

If anything happens to you while abroad, call those local numbers. You can get started right away to replace a lost or stolen passport, for example. In the meantime, *never* carry your passport or visa in a purse or wallet: If your pocket is picked or your bag is snatched, you'll lose your documents as well as your credit cards and money. Instead, carry your passport in a separate pocket. Better yet, get a zippered leg wrap or waist wrap that goes under your clothing.

Magellan's, a mail order company (call 800-962-4943), sells security wallets that can be tucked inside your clothing, through a belt loop, and neck pouches that hang by a cord. (Always wear such neck pouches *inside* your clothing.) Prices range from $10 to $20.

In Case of Emergency

If you're in an accident or are taken ill while you're out of the United States, you may need cash up front. Your health insurance card may not be accepted; Medicare generally won't pay for hospital or medical services outside the United States and its territories. Managed-care providers, such as health maintenance organizations (HMOs), and preferred provider organizations (PPOs) may in fact offer either *partial* or *no* coverage in foreign countries! Check with your insurer before you go. You might be able to buy, at a modest cost, a short-term rider that will cover you while you're traveling.

Also check with your credit card issuers. Many of them provide a phone number you can call to reach a "travel assistance company," if necessary. These companies fill a variety of roles: They might help you find a lawyer while overseas, or straighten out a dispute over a damaged rental car, for example.

Perhaps most important is the fact that travel assistance companies offer medical consulting service twenty-four hours a day. They can help find a doctor, or arrange for medical evacuation. Who'll pay?

That will depend on both your own health insurance and on the specific offer of the credit card company.

You should know too that if there are gaps in your foreign healthcare coverage, several companies can offer you travel insurance that's recognized around the world:

• TravMed/Medex Assistance (800-732-5309). Founded in 1977, this company sells coverage by the day for medical and hospital expenses. As of this writing, $3 per day was the standard fee, while students paid $2 and people over seventy paid $5. There are however limits on coverage for *preexisting conditions*—i.e., conditions that required treatment sometime in the previous ninety days are *not* covered.

• Europ Assistance Worldwide Services/Travel Assistance International (800-821-2828). Founded in 1963, this company sells evacuation coverage, local ambulance service, and emergency care. Individual and family coverage is priced per trip, depending upon the length. For example, a family vacation for up to fifteen days would be covered for $75, at last report. Again, there *are* restrictions on preexisting conditions. Travel agents frequently sell this coverage.

• International SOS Assistance (800-523-8930). Founded in 1975, it specializes in medical emergencies and evacuation, with *no* exclusions for preexisting conditions. For a couple on a fourteen-day trip, coverage is $60. Medical expense insurance is available for an extra charge.

• USAssist (800-756-5900). Founded in 1988, it specializes in medical evacuation; medical expenses are not covered. Annual membership cost $95 as of this writing, with *some* restrictions on preexisting conditions.

• Access America (800-284-8300). Founded in 1985, it offers services that include emergency medical and dental benefits. A family taking a two-week trip would pay $69 for a package of legal, medical, and trip-cancellation insurance; for an extra $30, baggage- and travel accident insurance can be included.

Generally, these services also will provide emergency cash, translation services, medical referrals, and links to U.S. doctors. These companies usually maintain twenty-four-hour hotlines. Callers will reach a staff member who, in turn, will make doctors' appointments, hospitalization arrangements, and (if necessary), air evacuation reservations to the nearest approved medical facility.

Deep Trouble

Consider what happened to Robert B., a Virginia-based consultant to the defense industry who went scuba diving in the Cayman Islands. Even though he observed the recommended safety rules, he wound up with a case of the "bends," a potentially fatal buildup of nitrogen bubbles in the bloodstream.

Fortunately, Robert had purchased catastrophe coverage from Access America. When informed of his sickness, the company arranged for him to be flown in a specially pressurized plane with a doctor and nurse to Duke University (in North Carolina) for emergency treatment. The cost for the air evacuation alone was $14,000: if Robert hadn't been covered by Access America, he would have had to find that much cash, up front, before the plane would take off.

A similar success story was told by Samuel T., who suffered an intestinal perforation and infection while spending the winter with his wife at their condo in St. Croix, in the U.S. Virgin Islands. Two operations were needed which could not be handled at the local hospital.

Sam was covered by a contract bought from Medical Air Services Association (MASA), through their condo development. He was able to fly first to Florida, then back to his home in New York, where he received the treatment he needed. The insurance policy not only helped him to get treatment, but also saved him nearly $8,000 in travel costs.

MASA (800-989-6272) specializes in expatriates and long-term foreign travelers, selling policies that are a bit more expensive than those offered by other emergency services (Sam and his wife paid $240) but last for at least one year. Family policies cover both spouses, as well as dependent children up to the age of twenty-three.

No matter what your insurance situation, call the Center for Disease Control & Prevention's hotline at 404-332-4559 before you travel outside the United States. The Center will tell you what food- and water precautions you need to take, which vaccinations are required, the diseases you might encounter, and type of preventive medicine recommended.

If you need a special vaccine, and your own physician is not familiar with it, you can seek out a travel-medicine practitioner. To get a list of over 100 specialists, send a large, self-addressed envelope and 98 cents in postage to Travelers Health & Immunization Service, 148 Highland Ave., Newton, MA 02165.

SUMMING UP

• Although no area of the world is perfectly safe, remember that some are extremely dangerous. The U.S. State Department maintains a phone hotline to inform travelers about which destinations are the most perilous.

• Before you leave the United States, make sure someone at home has the numbers of your passport, visa, credit cards, etc., to help you replace them in case of loss or theft.

• Always keep travel documents in a secure pocket, away from your cash or traveler's checks.

• Your domestic health insurance may not cover you outside the United States, but several services offer short-term insurance that can provide emergency medical service while you're in a foreign country.

• The Center for Disease Control & Prevention provides a hotline to tell travelers about special health hazards, but you may have to consult a travel-medical specialist to get the proper vaccinations and preventive treatment.

Part V

Healthy, Wealthy, Wise

14

Be Dollar-Wise,
Not Penny-Foolish

The Sensible Way to Cope With
Skyrocketing Health Insurance Costs

As of this writing, national health-care legislation was still very much up for debate—but likely in the end to take effect only on a state-by-state basis, with full implementatjon not required until the late 1990s, if then. In the meantime, don't neglect coverage for yourself and your family. Medical bills continue to soar, and one major illness or accident could wipe you out. Chances are, your employer now offers (or eventually will) *several* plans to choose among. (If you're self-employed, or if your employer doesn't provide health insurance, you'll have to buy your own coverage.)

Focus First on HMOs

Health maintenance organizations (HMOs) offer prepaid health care—you pay so much per person or per family, in return for virtually unlimited care, at little or no extra cost. Generally, HMOs are the least expensive choice for patients. For example, a 1992 study by the federal Bureau of Labor Statistics estimated that a family of four with an employer-paid premium and health-care expenses of around $7,000 would pay about $1,200 in out-of-pocket costs with traditional health insurance. That same family would pay less than $200 in an HMO.

But don't sign up for an HMO until you have looked at:

• *Doctors.* Are you willing to use the HMO's doctors? Are they mostly board-certified and well-regarded, with all specialties represented?

• *Hospitals.* Find out where you'll be sent in case of an operation or an emergency.

• *Locations.* If you have to go to one central HMO office, find out if it's convenient for you. Other HMOs use doctors who practice in their own offices, but make sure some of those physicians are near where you live or work.

• *Flexibility.* Some HMOs will let you go out of the network to see physicians, *if* you're willing to pay more of the cost. Instead of a $10 HMO visit, you might have to pay 20 percent of the doctor's bill.

• *Communications.* HMO patients who want answers to questions may face a daunting obstacle course of telephone transfers. See if there's a separate phone line for customer service.

• *Reach.* If your children are college students or future collegians, will the HMO provide coverage while they're away at school? Ideally, your kids should be able to get emergency care, then file a claim with your HMO.

• *Appointment time.* In a typical HMO, patients must first see a family doctor, or "gatekeeper," who'll make a referral to a specialist, if necessary. Unfortunately, family doctors are in short supply, so getting an appointment can be difficult. And when you're sick, you want to be able to see a doctor *immediately*.

• *Referral time.* You may be required to call a central office to clear referrals to specialists, schedule appointments, and discuss coverage. You're better off if your gatekeeper can make arrangements directly, saving you the hassle.

• *Physician screening.* Some HMOs aggressively keep tabs on doctors' performance, disciplining or even dropping those who receive a lot of patient complaints, fail to give patients the proper immunizations, and so on. *Don't* take an HMO's word for physician quality or patient service; ask some patients. If you don't know any, ask the HMO for names of patients who'll be willing to talk with you.

• *Grievances*. There should be a formal procedure for resolving patient disputes, and the plan should report that over 75 percent are settled within a month.

• *Accreditation*. Out of more than 500 HMOs in the United States, as of this writing, fewer than 100 were accredited by the National Committee for Quality Assurance, an independent organization that checks physicians and patient records. Find out if a prospective HMO has this credential.

HealthPlan Management Services, a consulting firm, rates over 400 HMOs on price and quality. Here were the top ten for 1993:

1. Kaiser Foundation Health Plan, San Francisco
2. Kaiser Foundation Health Plan, Los Angeles
3. Harvard Community Health Plan, Boston
4. Group Health, Minneapolis
5. TakeCare Health Plan, San Francisco
6. HMO PA—U.S. Healthcare, Philadelphia
7. Group Health Cooperative, Seattle
8. PacifiCare of California, Los Angeles
9. Pilgrim Health Care, Boston
10. MedCenters Health Plan, Minneapolis

Preferred-Provider Network News

Preferred provider organizations (PPOs) offer more flexibility. If you can't find an HMO that offers adequate service, or if you don't like the physicians on the list, a PPO may be a viable choice.

PPO structures vary, but the idea is to steer you to certain "providers" who have joined the network. If you see *those* providers, your financial exposure (deductibles, copayments) is less than if you go outside the network. Fees may be lower, too.

Again, there's an accrediting board—this time the American Accreditation Program—which has approved over 100 of the estimated 500 PPOs in the U.S.

Flying First Class

If you're willing to pay the price, the traditional "indemnity" system offers the most flexibility in choosing doctors. You can use *any* doctor and be reimbursed by the insurance company—paid back, that is, *after* you have satisfied your deductible and copayment requirements.

When you choose an indemnity plan (also called *fee-for-service*), choose real insurance rather than prepaid health care. That is, buy high-deductible insurance—$1,000 or $2,500 per person. With such plans, you pay most of your own doctor bills. You can even shop around and negotiate fees in advance. *Only* if you have a serious illness or injury will the insurance kick in.

The cost of this kind of real insurance is much less than the cost of low-deductible insurance—perhaps thousands of dollars less. If you and your family are reasonably healthy, you'll come out way ahead. Plus, you'll avoid the hassles of trying to get reimbursed for every $300 office visit. Be sure your fee-for-service plan has a stop-loss and a high cap on benefits. That is, after you pay $5,000 or so in any year, the insurance should take over and pay *all* your ongoing costs, up to at least $1 million.

Your employer may offer you a great deal on a low-deductible fee-for-service plan. But if you're buying your own insurance, such plans are out of reach.

For example, John H. was a corporate employee with first-rate health insurance: After he paid a $250 deductible, the plan picked up all the costs for his family of four. Then he left the company to start his own business, and found himself responsible for his own health insurance, too.

Even paying group rates—federal law forced his employer to let him continue coverage for sixteen months—he was paying $480 a month, nearly $6,000 per year. Individual coverage would have been even more expensive. So John raised his deductible to $2,000 and agreed to a 50 percent copayment, which means that after $2,000 he still pays half the bills. After paying a total of $7,000 per year, though, the stop-loss kicks in and the insurance takes over. The cost for this coverage was $350 per month in 1993, or $4,200 per year.

The bottom line: John and his family save at least $2,000 per year in insurance premiums, and probably much more. As long as they stay healthy, they're ahead of the game. The most they can be out of pocket is $7,000 per year, and they have protection against a catastrophic illness or disease.

Short-term fee-for-service plans are available for people who are between jobs, and for young adults no longer eligible for parental coverage but not yet entitled to employer coverage. Six-month plans, sold by insurers such as Golden Rule and Time Insurance, might cost only half as much as a standard plan. The catch: They generally don't cover preexisting conditions, so you're basically buying coverage only for new health problems that occur during this specific time frame.

In the Mainstream

Find out whether your physicians' fees are considered "usual and customary" before signing up for a fee-for-service plan. If a surgeon charges $125 for a consultation and your insurance company says it considers $75 to be a reasonable fee, you'll owe the extra $50, over and above any deductible or copayment and regardless of any stop-loss.

For $2–$4 per minute, you can call the Health Care Cost Hotline (900–225-2500) to learn the median fee, and range of fees, nationwide for more than 7,000 medical procedures. Two magazines, *Medical Economics* (201-945-9058) and *Health Pages* (212-929-6131), report on doctor fees by specialty, region, and type of service. You can compare your doctor's fees with the norm.

If your physicians' fees are way over the norm, they may be over your insurer's payment schedule, too. You may be better off in an HMO, with different physicians.

Relief in Sight

There may be low-cost alternatives if you're in a fee-for-service plan. For minor illnesses, X-rays, etc., consider seeing a Nurse Practitioner (NP)—typically a nurse with a master's degree. More than 30,000 NPs practice in the United States, either in their own offices, in clinics, or in doctors' offices. NPs charge rather less than doctors (perhaps 40 percent less, in some cases). Twenty states require insurers to reimburse NPs; in other states, many insurers cover NP services without a mandate to do so.

In addition to NPs, Physician Assistants (PAs) can handle most routine medical functions, thanks to a two-year training program. They earn about half what MDs earn, so their fees are commensurately lower.

Therefore, if you're in a fee-for-service plan, and you want to reduce your out-of-pocket expenses, ask your doctor if you can see an NP or PA, if available—concerning checkups, colds, and other non-critical appointments. If your doctor doesn't use NRPs or PAs, consider hunting for a doctor who does.

SUMMING UP

• Although federal health-care coverage may be in your future, for now you still have to provide your own protection—particularly if you're self-employed or work for an employer that does not provide health insurance.

• Your lowest-cost choice is probably a health-maintenance organization (HMO), which provides unlimited care for a predetermined fee.

• Before signing up for an HMO, be sure that it has a full range of doctors, convenient to where you live and work, and that it enjoys a good reputation among the patients who are enrolled.

• Traditional health insurance, in which you can go to any doctor, is increasingly expensive, so to lower premiums you should choose a high deductible—perhaps $2,000 or higher.

• Be sure your fee-for-service plan has a stop-loss that limits your out-of-pocket costs per year.

• If you're in a fee-for-service plan, you can cut costs by seeing Nurse Practitioners or Physician Assistants for routine services.

15

The Feds Fill the Medigap

Health Insurance for the
Social Security Set

When you reach age sixty-five, you qualify for *Medicare*, a federal health-insurance program, *regardless* of your health. It covers most medical bills—but not all. For example, patients are responsible for 20 percent of their doctors' bills. And, on long hospital stays, patients must (after 60 days) pay up to hundreds of dollars per day. Other exposures exist, too—usually modest, but occasionally catastrophic. To fill the gaps, *Medigap* insurance, sold by many insurers, was created. Over twenty-three million Americans spend more than $15 billion per year on Medigap insurance!

However, there was a great deal of confusion in the market. Insurers were offering a blizzard of different policies with relatively meaningless distinctions among them. They were difficult for buyers to compare and evaluate. Because the commission structure (naturally) rewarded agents for new sales much more than for renewals, many consumers bought policies when they already *had* adequate coverage. In fact, some consumers wound up with *several* policies.

Congress, gracious under pressure, finally passed a law calling for reform of the entire industry—which therapy took effect in 1992. Under the new law, the National Association of Insurance Commissioners (NAIC) came up with ten policies (see below). Every company that wants to sell Medigap insurance must offer A, the low-cost "core" policy. Insurers also can sell any or all of the other nine policies, B through J. No other Medigap policies can be sold, except in a few states with slightly different rules.

Standardized Medigap Policies

Medigap Policies

Benefits	A	B	C	D	E	F	G	H	I	J
Basic benefits	x	x	x	x	x	x	x	x	x	x
Part A hospital deductible		x	x	x	x	x	x	x	x	x
Skilled nursing home copayment			x	x	x	x	x	x	x	x
Part B deductible			x			x				x
Excess doctor charges (Part B)						(1)	(2)		(1)	(1)
Foreign travel emergency			x	x	x	x	x	x	x	x
At-home recovery				x			x		x	x
Outptient prescription drugs								(3)	(3)	(4)
Preventive screening					x					x

(1) 100%　　　　(3) maximum benefit $1,250
(2) 80%　　　　(4) maximum benefit $3,000

Note: Not all benefits are sold in every state.

Spelling Protection, A to J

Policy A covers the most common exposures:

• Such policies must pay the big hospital bills not covered by Medicare. Patients are liable for $174 per day (in 1994) for days 61 through 90, and $348 per day for a further 60 "lifetime reserve days." Core policies cover these costs plus full payments for an additional 365 days.

• Such policies must pay the 20 percent coinsurance for medical

expenses—especially doctor's bills—that Medicare requires from patients.

Policy B adds coverage for the Medicare Part A deductible, set at
$696 per benefit period in 1994. That is, if you have this coverage,
the policy pays the first $696 for hospital stays in each benefit period;
with Policy A, the patient is responsible for the first $696.

All other policies, *C through J*, pay the Medicare Part A deductible.
Also, each of these policies pays benefits for skilled nursing homes
and for medical expenses incurred while traveling outside the United
States. Medicare picks up *all* costs for the first twenty days in an
approved nursing facility, but patients owe $87 for each of the next
eighty days (1994 rate). This exposure, nearly $7,000, is worth cov-
ering. Also, foreign travel is a major exposure for Medicare recipients.
If you're traveling out of the country, even only to Canada or Mexico,
your medical expenses there probably *aren't* covered by Medicare.
Therefore, you probably should go beyond policy A if you can afford
a few hundred dollars more per year.

Some of the other optional benefits, such as preventive care and
the $100 doctor-bill deductible, relate to meager exposures that
needn't be covered. The at-home recovery feature has somFe value,
but there's a benefit cap: Reimbursement is pegged at up to $40 per
visit, up to $1,600 per year. You may have to buy some of these
features, though, in order to get more valuable protection.

Prime Choices

How should you choose from among policies C through J? There are
two key screens: *prescription drugs* and *balance billing*.

Are you likely to need several thousand dollars' worth of prescription drugs a year? With policies H and I you pay the first $250, then
the policy pays 50 percent, up to a $1,250 annual limit. Policy J works
the same, except that the upper limit is $3,000.

Balance billing is more complicated. Medicare sets limits on certain
medical procedures and pays 80 percent; all ten Medigap policies pay
the other 20 percent coinsurance. If the Medicare limit on hip re-
placements is $2,000, for example, Medicare will pay $1,600 while a
Medigap policy will pay $400.

However, not all doctors stick with the Medigap limits. Any excess
is called *balance billing*, which is the patient's responsibility. Although

federal legislation caps balance billing for Medicare patients, a hip replacement (for example) might cost $2,200, leaving a $200 hole to fill.

This may not be a problem. Some Northeastern states have banned balance billing, or are moving in that direction. In some other areas of the country, medical fees usually are low, so balance billing isn't a significant problem.

Here's how to play the Medigap game:

• If you likely will spend much more than $3,000 on prescription drugs a year, buy J. No matter *what* sort of health condition you're in, you can take advantage of the open enrollment period and buy this policy within six months of signing up for Medicare Part B. Then, the Medigap policy will pay for up to $3,000 worth of prescription drugs a year.

• If your drug need is smaller, but still well over $1,000 per year, H or I may be the best bet. Choose I if there's likely to be a balance billing problem, H if balance billing isn't a concern.

• If you don't anticipate a heavy reliance on prescription drugs and you may run into a balance billing problem, G looks like the best choice because at-home recovery is included. (Remember, the difference between 80 percent and 100 percent of balance billing might be only 2 percent of the total bill.) Policy F might be worthwhile if it's well-priced.

• If you're neither a heavy user of prescription drugs nor vulnerable to balance billing, you can choose from the cheapest policies, C through J, and provide good catastrophic protection.

Some experts have indicated that D, F, and H may be good value-for-money choices. When you compare prices among policies, check the insurer's *premium schedules*, which are also known as the *outlines of coverage*. Find out if premiums will remain relatively stable, or will rise each year (due to your increasing age). You might be better off with a policy that's more expensive now, rather than one whose premiums will escalate in the future. Some worthwhile lower-cost group policies may be available through social or professional organizations you might do well to become more familiar with.

Ask if an insurer offers electronic billing, which could save you money and reduce aggravation. Also, some insurers offer *crossover billing*—automatic claims handling via which Medicare bills go directly to the Medigap insurance company. With this system, policyholders won't pay bills and then forget to file for reimbursement—which, strange to say, frequently happens.

Window of Opportunity

Another aspect of these Medigap rules is a *six-month window*, open for that long after one enrolls in Medicare Part B (generally at age 65). During this grace period, any qualified person can buy any of the new policies, regardless of his or her health. Even if you have a medical problem, you'll *still* be able to choose the *most* comprehensive policies. This "adverse selection," as the insurance companies put it, will most benefit the most severely ill—*if* they act wisely in the given time period. Coverage of preexisting conditions *can't* be excluded on new policies, and *must* be covered on replacement policies.

A few other features are built into the system. For example: Medigap policies must be *guaranteed* renewable (except because of non-payment of premiums, or misrepresentation), which means they *can't* be cancelled willy-nilly. This rule limits the spread between commissions on new and replacement policies, with rewards to encourage persistency—consumers renewing policies for many years. In some states, selling a replacement policy will generate a renewal commission, *not* a new-policy commission. The aim is to stop "churning," which we ran into earlier on.

Here's another built-in feature: The *minimum loss ratio* has been raised from 60 percent to 65 percent. Thus, at least 65 percent of premiums received *must* be paid out in claims. In addition, the guidelines prescribe a specific formula for arriving at the loss ratio, which will make it easier to enforce this requirement and harder for insurance companies to play around with their numbers. (Figures can't lie, but liars can figure.) If an insurance company doesn't meet the 65 percent test, its policyholders will get a credit equivalent to the shortfall.

Finally, disclosure forms have been reworked which explain how the policies compare. All buyers *must* receive these forms. They show (e.g.) that *duplicate* policies are now *illegal*: Companies and agents can't sell them, so won't unless they're willing to risk fines of up to $25,000 per policy.

Price Isn't Everything

Now that policies are standardized, how can you best choose from among Medigap insurers? On *price*, of course. Why buy a Policy A for say $600 when you can buy the same coverage for perhaps $375? (Actual prices may vary widely from company to company.) But don't shop on price *alone*. You might for instance want to spend a little more to buy from an insurer with an excellent reputation and extraordinary financial strength. You'll also want an insurer who emphasizes service, including speedy approval of applications, swift responses to customer questions, and rapid claims processing.

Most insurers will honor old, prestandard policies *as long as you are thereafter willing to renew*. In some cases these older policies offer greater benefits or better all-around values. So go over both the old and new policies carefully before deciding on changing.

In about a dozen states—prominently including California, Florida, and Texas—you can mix HMOs with a Medigap policy. You get the same coverage as any Medigap policy, but you pay about 15 percent–20 percent less because you sign up for Medicare Select, and thus agree to use only certain doctors and hospitals. In Florida, for example, a sixty-eight-year-old man buying a standard Medigap policy from Blue Cross and Blue Shield might pay $85 per month, but only $70 a month with the Blue Cross/Blue Shield Medicare Select policy.

If you shop hard enough, you can find above-average health-insurance protection for below-average costs!

Recovery Room

No matter *what* kind of health insurance you have, if you wind up in a hospital, you'll wind up paying *some* part of your bills. Sometimes your out-of-pocket expenses, for example, will be modest, while some other patients will end up owing thousands of dollars on them. At least that's what the *hospitals* say. According to insurance company auditors, more than 90 percent of all hospital bills contain errors, and two-thirds of those miscues are in the hospitals' favor! It's a lot easier to double-charge a patient for certain items than to forget to bill for something.

You don't have to take hospital overcharges lying down—or in whatever other position they've left you. *Always* ask for a completely itemized bill, and question doubtful entries. Be *aware* of duplicate charges—two catheters rather than one, for example. To help your memory, either you or someone responsible to (or for) you can keep a log during your hospital stay.

If you spot any errors, complain at *once*. That's what Karen S. of Tampa did after she was billed $8,700 for a jaw operation that had an "estimated maximum cost" of $7,000. She objected to paying $28 for liquid protein she never received, $75 for two tubes of ointment selling in drugstores for $5 each, and so on.

She protested to the hospital's billing department, which knocked more than $400 off her bill. *Still* not satisfied, she wrote a formal complaint letter to the Florida Health Care Cost Containment Board, which leaned on the hospital to forgive another $1,300. Karen saved $1,700 altogether, bringing her total cost back down to the $7,000 estimate.

If you're going to be hospitalized, spend a few dollars to join the People's Medical Society (215-770-1670). Not only will you get help deciphering your bill, but you'll receive leads about where to complain if you spot overcharges.

Hospital patients scheduled for surgery have an even more important concern: contaminated blood transfusions. If possible, stock your own blood in a blood bank before any operation. Another option is to select a hospital that uses a "cell saver," which circulates your own blood back into your body during surgery.

SUMMING UP

• Americans over age sixty-five are covered by Medicare, but Medicare has gaps.

• To fill Medicare gaps, seniors should have Medigap insurance, which now is strictly regulated by federal law.

• Although low-cost core policies provide basic coverage, some more-expensive Medigap policies offer such valuable benefits as prescription drugs and coverage while traveling abroad.

• Be sure to apply for a Medigap policy soon after you become eligible for Medicare Part B, at age sixty-five, because you'll be able to buy *any* policy, *regardless* of your health.

• Hospital bills frequently contain overcharges, but you can win reductions with persistent protests.

16

Dealing With Disability

How to Protect Your Income Stream If You Can't Work

James R. wasn't worried. He was thirty-six, in perfect health, and running his own construction business. Then, with no warning, he suffered a major heart attack and had to close his company. He applied for other construction jobs, but couldn't pass the physical exam. He and his wife went through their $70,000 savings account in a few years.

Unhappily, James's experience is all too common. According to Price Waterhouse, workers between ages thirty-five and sixty-five are six times as likely to be disabled as they are to die; the U. S. Housing and Home Finance Agency reports that 48 percent of mortgage foreclosures result from disability, versus 3 percent from death. Although you probably won't be comfortable thinking about it, disability is a risk you need to face.

If you get sick or hurt, your health insurance will pay the doctor and hospital bills. But who'll pay *you* if you can't work for a long time period? For that you need *disability insurance.*

Disability insurance paid off for Durwood W., who owned half of a computer distributorship whose annual sales were around $1 million. Back in 1981, when Durwood was forty-two, an aneurism in his brain burst. The surgeons removed a blood clot and gave him a 50 percent chance of survival. He survived, but his reading acumen had dropped from college level to second grade—so his career as an executive was over.

Since then, Durwood has been turned down for Social Security disability benefits three times. Fortunately, however, he and his company had purchased *disability income policies.* The company policy replaced his salary for a year, after which his personal policy kicked in. In addition, the company policy paid Durwood's partners a lump sum, so they could buy out his share of the firm. Thanks to these policies, income kept coming in, and Durwood's wife was able to stay home with their three daughters—all of whom were able to go through college.

Similarly, Dr. David R., a neurologist in Massachusetts, lost his ability to practice medicine in 1991, after he was struck by a van while riding his bike on a short, normally safe trip to a store. He suffered severe head injuries, and spent thirteen days in a coma.

David's disability insurance allowed him to maintain his mortgage payments while his wife finished her medical residency. His family continues to live comfortably. Moreover, David had a *business overhead disability policy*, which paid the rent as well as employee salaries, keeping his practice intact until he could sell it.

A Friend in Need

The premise of disability insurance is simple: If you can't work because of illness or injury, your income will drop, and perhaps disappear altogether. Nevertheless, you'll still have ongoing expenses. In such cases, disability insurance will pick up either some or all of the slack. A disability policy will pay you a certain amount *each month* if you can't work. When you buy disability insurance, you pay a smaller or larger premium in order to buy a commensurately smaller or larger monthly benefit.

You may think you already have disability coverage from your employer. Check on it! Many group disability policies last only six months or so. That won't save you from a financial catastrophe if you can't work for a year or more.

If you have no employer coverage, or if your group coverage is inadequate, you need to buy disability insurance on your own. You may find it difficult to afford the increased premiums, especially if you're struggling to meet all your other bills. The answer, in many cases, is to cut back on coverage—especially the "extras" that often are sold with such policies.

To hold costs down, insure only against *catastrophic* risks. Here, the real risk is that you'll have a lengthy disability that destroys your earning power. Focus on that protection, and ignore unnecessary options.

Your first task is to determine how much coverage you need. Insurers usually say to cover 60 percent–70 percent of your income. If you make $60,000 per year, which is $5,000 per month, you're advised to buy a policy that pays $3,000–$3,500 per month.

But do you really need that much coverage? A policy that pays $2,000 per month will be much cheaper. Your living standard may decline, but you won't starve if you collect $24,000 per year, tax-free, in addition to investment income, other family members' earnings, and the like. Buying a low-benefit policy is better than buying a more expensive policy you won't be able to keep in force.

Trimming the Fat

There's more to disability insurance than wrenched backs, strokes, and heart attacks. Claims for "mental and nervous" disorders, including drug and alcohol addictions, are increasingly common. And disability insurers, forced to foot the bill for all manner of stress-related claims, are becoming increasingly skeptical—looking harder than ever at applicants these days. For example, poor health risks are being either rejected or asked to pay higher premiums. You're likely to find that disability insurance, always pricey, is more and more so.

Whether you're buying a stand-alone disability policy or a supplement to group coverage, you'll find that disability insurance is expensive, costing 2 percent–3 percent of your income per year, or even more. A forty-year-old who wants to buy disability coverage with a $5,000 monthly benefit probably will pay premiums of around $2,000 per year, depending on policy features.

To keep your costs down, *don't* buy all the costly extras your agent may recommend. These add-ons could prove valuable, but you can do without them and still achieve your goal of financial security in case of long-term disability. For example, you can cut your premium by loosening up on the definition of disability. The basic policy is "any occupation" (any-occ), covering conditions under which you can't do the work you're suited for by reason of education and training.

Recently, disability insurers have been pushing more-expensive "own occupation" coverage (own-occ) that will pay if you can't perform your specific job duties. The classic example is a surgeon who hurts his hand, so takes a less lucrative job teaching: He'd collect under an own-occ policy, but not under an any-occ policy.

However, most people don't have such special circumstances. Own-occ, which is much more expensive, is "really a marketing-driven thing," a life-insurance executive told the *Wall Street Journal*. People feed their egos by buying own-occ and telling themselves that they're worth it.

In truth, most white-collar professionals are well-served by a disability policy that will pay if they can't perform suitable work. Make sure you go over a policy's definition of disability before you consider buying!

Choose a ninety-day waiting period before benefits begin. Your true risk is long-term disability, not three months without pay. Going from a thirty-day to ninety-day waiting period might save you 45 percent in premiums!

At the other end of the spectrum, buy a policy that pays until age sixty-five, not for your lifetime. Buying lifetime benefits can increase your premium by 75 percent because insurance companies are worried about the length of their exposure. Even if you're still disabled at sixty-five, and your insurance benefits stop, you'll be able to collect Social Security and other retirement benefits.

If you have a disability policy that pays after a 90-day waiting period, until age sixty-five, you're protected against disasters.

Offers You Can Refuse

Another option you can avoid is a *return-of-premium* feature. With this option, you'll get all or part of your money back, ten or twenty years from now, depending on the extent of the benefits you have received.

This "money-back" offer sounds great, but such policies may in fact cost 50 percent more. And they don't address the *key* reason for buying this insurance: protecting yourself against long-term disability.

Similarly, you probably can do without a *cost-of-living* rider. Say you buy a $5,000-a-month disability insurance policy with a COLA. If you're disabled, your monthly benefit will go up to $5,300, $5,500, etc., in sync with increases in inflation.

Again, this certainly is desirable, but the cost may be excessive. For someone in their forties, a COLA can increase the annual premium by 40 percent. Is that worth an extra 5 percent or 10 percent per year, as of some unknown future date?

Moreover, if you are disabled for a long period, your biggest headache may be making your mortgage payments so you can keep your house. You won't need a COLA for that because mortgage payments will usually be fixed, or at least will not rise above the cap on an adjustable-rate mortgage.

Rather than paying up for a COLA, you're better off adjusting your coverage every few years, as your circumstances change. Some companies will sell you a low-cost rider that enables you to buy extra coverage without a medical exam.

There is another option that generally is worth buying: *residual disability*. With this feature, you'll get a partial disability benefit if you can work only part-time.

Suppose, for example, you buy a disability insurance policy paying $5,000 per month. You suffer a heart attack that cuts in half your ability to work, and trims your income by 50 percent. The policy would pay you $2,500 per month, in addition to what you earn. With a good residual disability rider, you won't need own-occ coverage, because you're protected against loss of income.

Another wrinkle worth buying is a "Social Security" rider. If you don't qualify for Social Security disability benefits (most applicants are rejected), this rider will increase your benefit by, say, $1,000 per month. The cost of this rider is far less than buying an extra $1,000 in basic monthly benefits.

If you're a business owner, ask about special coverage. Some insurers have policies that will fund a buy–sell agreement if you're disabled, or the company's overhead expense may be covered while you're not working and not bringing in business.

Always be sure that disability insurance, like health- or life insurance, is "guaranteed renewable." This means that your coverage can't be dropped as long as you keep paying the premiums, even if your health deteriorates.

Discounts on Demand

Most insurers quote lower rates for nonsmokers than for nicotine enthusiasts. That's one way to cut premiums. Ask if an insurer also offers *annual renewable disability insurance* (ARDI), a little-publicized form of disability insurance in which premiums start out low—perhaps 50 percent of the basic price—and increase each year. This makes the most sense if you expect your annual income to increase. Agents don't push ARDI, perhaps because commissions are lower, but it may be a good way to buy disability insurance at a price you can afford, so perhaps you should check it out.

When you shop for disability insurance, you may discover that underwriting criteria are being toughened up in terms of finances, too. Previously, many companies would accept your word about your income. Increasingly, insurers are insisting on seeing tax returns and other financial documents. Some have hired CPAs to assist in underwriting, while others offer discounts to buyers who provide full financial disclosure.

Why is this so important? Disability insurers will offer benefits up to around only 60 percent of income. If you report $10,000 in monthly income, for example, you might be able to buy a policy paying $6,000 in monthly disability benefits. However, if you actually have $5,000 in monthly income, you could be sorely tempted to pay the premiums for a while, discover a "disability," and collect increased income while not working at all.

The tax consequences of disability benefits are straightforward. If *you* paid the premiums, benefits are tax-free. If your *employer* paid the premiums, benefits are taxable. In case of a split-dollar arrangement, a pro rata share will be taxed.

Some corporations offer employees "cafeteria" or "flex" benefit programs incorporating a selection of fringe benefits. If you have the opportunity to participate in such a plan, choose to have the *company* fund other fringes while *you* pay disability costs. Any disability benefits you receive will then be tax-free.

Now for the Hard Part

Buying the right policy at the right price isn't everything. You need to buy from a reputable insurer, and you need to pay attention to the exact terms of the policy.

Trial lawyer Lawrence H., for example, was stricken with multiple sclerosis, which made it difficult for him to speak—and so he couldn't try cases. He had disability coverage, but when he filed his initial claim, he didn't include a medical certificate from a physician. The insurance company refused to pay because of this technicality, forcing Lawrence to sue for benefits.

Similar difficulties faced Larry Z., a fifty-seven-year-old engineer who suffered severe head injuries when he was hit by a car in his company parking lot. For the next year and a half, Larry tried to work, even though his short-term memory was so bad that he had to tape-record instructions from his boss. Eventually he had a bout of vertigo, fell in a stairwell, and sustained brain damage. By the time Larry applied for disability benefits, his insurer turned him down because he had worked for 180 days after the auto injury. Again, his claim wound up in litigation.

Sometimes, however, disability claimants prevail in court. Pamela B., for example, a forty-one-year-old accountant who lost income after neck surgery, had her disability claim rejected. The insurer said she hadn't disclosed headaches, fatigue, allergies, back pain, sinus problems, and athlete's foot when she applied for a policy. She went to court, and a jury agreed that the insurance company should not have rescinded her policy over such trivial and irrelevant conditions. Pamela got her benefits, her attorney's fees, and a $25,000 award.

But you can't rely on a court victory, and you don't want to subject yourself to that trouble and expense unnecessarily. So check into the insurance company before buying: Companies with top ratings from A. M. Best, Moody's, and Standard & Poor's are more likely to pay claims without a hassle. Even with reputable companies, though, you should make full disclosure on your disability insurance application, and follow the claims-filing procedures carefully.

SUMMING UP

• If you can't work, your income will shrink while your ongoing expenses continue.

• Disability insurance will pay you a monthly benefit to help you meet your living expenses.

• Disability insurance is expensive, so buy only as much coverage as you'll need to ward off disaster.

• To cut costs, stipulate a long waiting period before benefits begin, and an end of benefits at age sixty-five—when you'd be retiring even if not disabled.

• You can do without such expensive options as specialized "own-occupation" coverage, cost-of-living adjustments, and money-back offers in case benefits aren't claimed.

• Some features are worthwhile—for example, a residual disability option that pays you partial benefits while your income is reduced.

• If you pay for a disability insurance policy yourself, any benefits you receive will be tax-free, so you should ask your employer to pay for other fringe benefits rather than for disability insurance.

• Deal with top-rated disability insurers, fill out applications honestly and thoroughly, and follow claims-filing procedures exactly.

17

Make Sure Your Money Doesn't Run Out Before You Do

Coping With the Crippling Costs of Long-Term Care

The cost of nursing-home stays has increased dramatically, reaching nearly $100,000 per year in some areas. Your wealth (or your inheritance from your parents or whomever) can be wiped out by a long spell in a nursing home. Therefore, *long-term care* (LTC) insurance, which will pay policyholders in case they're confined to a nursing home, has grown in popularity. From nowhere, in 1987, such policies now account for around $3 billion in premiums per year.

However, more that just a few buyers don't stick around: Consumer groups report that as many as 80 percent of all buyers allow LTC policies to lapse before they even receive any benefits! That's an astonishing lapse rate, considering that these policies are only a few years old.

Why the incredible dropout rate (which stat insurance companies challenge)? Because these policies are quite expensive. The average price of a policy purchased at age sixty-five is about $1,700 per year; for a topflight policy, the annual cost might be around $3,000. A married couple, of course, need to pay for *two* policies.

Apparently LTC policies are being oversold—to people who can't afford the ongoing premiums. After a few years, they let the coverage lapse. The National Association of Insurance Commissioners (NAIC), the umbrella group of state insurance commissioners, has agreed to *force* insurers to pay *some* benefits to consumers, even *after* policies lapse. The NAIC's Long-Term Care Insurance Model Act holds that "No long-term care insurance policy or certificate may be delivered . . . unless such policy or certificate provides for nonforfeiture benefits."

Better than Nothing

As of this writing, nonforfeiture benefits seemed destined to become standard in the mid- to late 1990s. Judging from the NAIC report, the most likely form of nonforfeiture benefit will be the *shortened benefit period*. That is, suppose a consumer buys an LTC policy that will pay $100 per day for up to three years. After a certain number of years, the consumer lets the policy lapse. With a shortened benefit period provision, the consumer might retain an LTC policy that will pay $100 per day for one or two years.

Another possible approach is to offer a *reduced paid-up* policy as a nonforfeiture provision. The holder of a policy with $100,000 in maximum benefits might get a $40,000 or $50,000 policy instead.

Insurance companies now offering these types of coverage generally charge 10 percent–30 percent higher premiums, compared with policies that do not have these features. According to the NAIC long-term care task force, providing nonforfeiture benefits could increase premiums by 7 percent–13 percent at issue age seventy-five, and 64 percent–232 percent (!) at issue age thirty-five. Although the task force implies that premium hikes might be reduced, it's clear that the costs of LTC coverage are going even higher.

Strength in Numbers

How can you hold down the costs? Buy through your employer's group policy, if one is offered. Such policies, which have to be approved by corporate benefits managers, often have better coverage than do individual policies. Typically, you can buy LTC insurance for your parents as well as for yourself and your spouse.

In a group plan, employees pay the premiums. Because prices are negotiated, premiums may be 20 percent–30 percent lower than for individual policies. And group LTC policies are *portable*, meaning that you can take yours with you if you leave your employer.

If you're not covered by a group plan, you *have* to buy individual LTC coverage. Here are some ways to hold down the costs of an LTC policy you buy on your own:

• *Buy young.* A policy bought at age forty-five might cost around $375 per year, whereas the same policy costs $1,700 per year if bought at age seventy. Your annual premium can't be raised unless the insurer raises it for *all* of its local policyholders.

• *Choose a lengthy waiting period.* Pay for the first 90 or 100 days in a nursing home yourself, before benefits kick in.

• *Limit your benefit period to three years.* That will give you enough time to transfer assets and qualify for Medicaid. Make sure you execute a durable power of attorney so your assets can be transferred if you're not capable of doing that (see Chapter 23).

• *Avoid home-care coverage.* Home-care coverage seems to be everybody's favorite: Who *wouldn't* prefer to spend his or her last days at home, covered by insurance (as well as given lots of personal attention), rather than in a nursing home? As a practical matter, though, your greatest risk of expensive custodial care is a long nursing-home stay rather than home health care.

Should you need year-after-year care, it's unlikely you'll be staying at home. You'll probably have to go into an institution. While home-care benefits frequently are bought in LTC policies, they're seldom used. Most people prefer to pay the $50 per day out of their own pocket, and save the $100 LTC insurance for the nursing home. So you may be better off skipping this expensive coverage, which could add 40 percent or more to your annual premium.

• *Don't buy a policy that will provide increasing benefits to protect against inflation.* You're paying in today's dollars for a benefit you may or may not receive years in the future.

Buy coverage that doesn't skimp on the essentials. An LTC policy should pay for custodial care, in any type of facility, with no prior hospitalization necessary. Benefits should be triggered if you can't perform such activities of daily living as bathing, dressing, and so on.

And there should be specific coverage for Alzheimer's and other organic-based mental illness.

If you're shopping for long-term care insurance, be sure to buy from a company that uses "front-end underwriting," screening applicants' health histories diligently. Such companies tend to insure healthier people so they'll be better able to hold down costs.

Back-end underwriters don't do much screening, so it's easier to get a policy. However, they likely will cover riskier clients, driving up costs, and they're more motivated to find inaccuracies in your initial application, so they can reject claims.

SUMMING UP

• As nursing home costs increase, LTC policies have become increasingly popular.
• Such policies pay a benefit if you need care in a nursing home, an expense not covered by Medicare or by private health insurance.
• Many LTC policies are allowed to lapse by consumers who don't keep up with the premiums.
• Insurance regulators have announced they'll *force* insurers to pay some benefits, even on lapsed policies.
• To cover this mandated expense, the cost of LTC policies will rise—perhaps substantially.
• You can keep LTC policies affordable by avoiding such extras as home-care coverage, inflation-adjusted benefits, and lifetime benefits.
• No matter how stringently you cut back, buy a policy from a reputable insurer that will cover stays in any type of nursing home, even without a prior hospital stay.

18

Winning the Endgame

How to Protect Your Parents' Savings— and Your Inheritance

Federal government statistics indicate that 4 percent of all men and 13 percent of all women can expect to spend at least five years in a nursing home. Having an aging parent confined to a nursing home is bad enough. Even worse is the prospect of seeing your family's assets evaporate, month after month, year after year. That modest inheritance you had hoped would help pay for your kids' college education or your own retirement may wind up in the pockets of a nursing-home operator.

An increasingly popular choice for financing nursing-home care is Medicaid, a federal–state welfare program. Nearly half of all U.S. nursing-home costs are paid by Medicaid.

To qualify for Medicaid, your aging parents must virtually impoverish themselves. They can have only a very limited income, and less than $2,000 in assets—plus (fortunately) a house, a car, and some personal possessions. Married couples can have nearly $75,000 in assets (as of 1994), plus the exclusions noted above. After they strip themselves down to that level, Medicaid will pay medical expenses, including nursing-home bills.

For these reasons, Medicaid "transfers" have become common. Your parents first give away enough assets (if they have enough to start with) to get down to the poverty line, *then* apply for Medicaid. Transfers may be outright—usually they're to relatives. Then those relatives will be responsible for supporting their elders for as long as no nursing-home care is needed. Or, Medicaid transfers can be to *trusts*. Then, the trustee (perhaps a child, perhaps a family friend or adviser) could pay out trust assets as necessary.

Wait Loss

You might think, "I'll wait until a parent goes into a nursing home, then arrange to transfer enough assets to the next generation to meet the Medicaid limits." That's certainly one strategy, but it has its costs.

Transferring assets creates a waiting period. A complicated formula (involving the amount transferred, and local nursing-home rates) is used to determine the length of the waiting period. During this time, someone else—probably the recipients of the transferred assets— has to pay nursing-home bills.

Suppose your father—let's say a widower—gives away $100,000 worth of assets in order to come down to the Medicaid limit. In his state, the average nursing-home cost is $4,000 per month. Thus, your father would have to wait twenty-five months ($100,000 ÷ $4,000) before Medicaid paid his medical expenses.

Until 1993, the waiting period was capped at thirty months. Whether your father gave away $150,000 or $1,000,000, he'd still be eligible after thirty months. Nowadays, the waiting period may be thirty-six months, or even longer (see below).

Besides the waiting period, there's another problem with using a wait-and-transfer strategy. Suppose your parent has to go into a nursing home because of a stroke or Alzheimer's, or some other ailment that renders him or her incompetent. An asset transfer might not be possible, and *all* your parent's assets will be on the line for nursing-home bills.

A different approach, then, is to transfer assets while your parents are still of sound body and mind. If they later are confined to a nursing home, the waiting period may have expired, and they'll be eligible for Medicaid immediately.

That may make good financial sense, but it's often not practical. Few elderly parents want to give away all of their assets so they can live out their lives in poverty, dependent on their children. If they never need to be institutionalized, they'll have gone through this turmoil for nothing.

Lack of Trust

Besides extending the waiting period from thirty to thirty-six months, the 1993 tax law changed the rules on Medicaid transfers in other respects:

• Anyone who sets up a trust fund must wait at least five years before applying to Medicaid.

• States may consider any distribution from a trust to be a transfer, starting a new waiting period. That applies even to trusts in existence before the law was passed.

• Premature Medicaid applications may wipe out the thirty-six-month cap. That is, if you apply after thirty-five months when you should have waited thirty-six months, your waiting period will be the full amount of assets divided by the monthly cost, even if that's 200 or 300 months.

• States are now required to recover outlays from the estates of Medicaid patients. This includes a principal residence, even if it was transferred to a spouse or a child.

Therefore, if you intend to do any Medicaid planning now, you're better off without using a trust. The new rules are clearly intended to put an end to the use of Medicaid trusts. If you have, or another family member already has, a trust in place, consult with an attorney before making any further distributions.

Deal From Strength

Medicaid planning is still viable if you're willing to make outright transfers and then wait up to thirty-six months. Of course, your parents must have absolute faith that the money will be provided as needed. Also: If you plan on having Medicaid pay for nursing-home expenses, be prepared to lose all or part of the sale proceeds from your parents' house, because your state likely will seek reimbursement.

The bottom line is that Medicaid planning should be used *only* as a last resort. Why should your aging parents impoverish themselves for the rest of their lives, giving up financial independence, on the chance that long-term nursing home care *might* be needed?

So—how can you keep your family wealth from this dilemma?

1. Have a frank talk with your parents. Discuss the costs of local nursing-home care, and the extent of their assets.

2. Hire an attorney who specializes in the emerging "elder law" area.

3. Have a durable power of attorney drawn up, giving someone in the next generation the authority to handle your parents' assets in case of their incompetency.

4. If long-term care insurance is available at a decent price, buy it. You want a policy that will cover custodial care in virtually all institutions. Choose a three-year benefit period, giving you time to transfer assets and outlast the waiting period. After the insurance runs out, Medicaid will take over.

5. If you can't buy insurance, plan a gradual, partial transfer of assets, beginning as soon as possible. The idea is to leave your parents enough so they maintain their independence, yet reduce the amount subject to nursing-home fees. The transfer might be to a trust, with a trustee in whom your parents have confidence. The trust *can* have the ability (but *can't* be required) to make distributions to your parents while they're not yet institutionalized.

6. Always leave your parents enough to enter a first-class nursing home as paying customers. Many good nursing homes won't take Medicaid patients, but few will actually discharge a patient who has been there for a while and run out of money. Check carefully on a nursing home before sending a parent there!

SUMMING UP

• Many people rely upon Medicaid to pay nursing home bills.
• Medicaid is a poverty program, so people have to impoverish themselves to qualify.
• If you wait to transfer assets, you'll run into a lengthy waiting period and have to pay nursing-home costs in the interim.
• If you arrange an asset transfer *beforehand*, when nursing-home care *isn't* required, you run the risk that the elderly person will have given up his or her independence needlessly.

• The 1993 tax law made it more difficult to transfer assets and qualify for Medicaid.

• You're better off buying a three-year, long-term care policy and executing a durable power of attorney, then arranging a Medicaid transfer only if a long nursing-home stay is inevitable.

Part VI

Keep Golden Years From Turning Leaden

19

Too Safe Can Be Sorry

Keep Your Retirement Funds From Evaporating

There was a time when retirement planning was fairly simple. You might work until age sixty-five and then live off your savings for a little while longer, or if lucky until your death. Back in 1935, when Social Security was passed into law, the average life expectancy was around sixty-one years. That's not the case anymore. People increasingly live for many years after they retire. Early retirement is becoming common, at age sixty-two, sixty, or even younger.

At the same time, life expectancy is steadily lengthening. In early 1994, *Fortune* magazine reported that the average life expectancy was 72.7 years for American men and 79.6 years for American women. According to mutual-fund sponsor T. Rowe Price, an individual who retires at age fifty-five has an average life expectancy of twenty-eight years. If that individual has a spouse, also age fifty-five, the combined life expectancy is thirty-four years.

Even if you wait until age sixty-five to retire, you can expect to live for another twenty years. If your spouse is also sixty-five, the combined life expectancy is twenty-five years. (Naturally, if your spouse is younger, the combined life expectancy is even greater.)

Remember, those are averages. Dr. Edward Schneider, head of the Andrus Gerontology Center at the University of Southern California, has predicted that "At least half the baby boomers [today's middle-aged people] might expect to live into their late eighties and nineties."

The Long Goodbye

After you retire, you're likely to spend *many* years with little or no earned income. You need to plan for twenty, twenty-five—even thirty—years of not working, or of working part-time. And that will take lots of money, if you're looking forward to a *comfortable* retirement.

How can you gauge what amount of money you'll need to maintain your standard of living after you stop working? If you're only a few years from retirement, you can use the *itemized budget analysis* method: Review your current expenses and see which ones you'll keep up after retirement, which you'll drop, which you'll increase, and so on. You'll get a pretty good idea of what your actual expenses will be.

But what if you're five or ten years from retirement? Or even farther away? The longer the time period until retirement, the more you'll have to estimate future cash needs.

Booke & Co., an employee benefits firm, has determined that most people will need about 70 percent of their adjusted preretirement income for the kind of retirement they'd like. For example:

Your 1995 household income	$60,000
Minus savings	5,000
Minus taxes paid	15,000
Result = Total living expenses	40,000
Multiplied by suggested replacement ratio of 70%	28,000

As the table shows, you'd need about $28,000 a year to live comfortably. That's *after taxes*, of course. Assume a 25 percent income-tax rate, and you come out with around $37,000 gross income necessary for a comfortable retirement. But that's in 1994 dollars. And most assuredly you'll find that $37,000 in say 2015 won't buy you nearly as much as in (for example) 1995. You need to adjust for inflation, using a table such as this:

Years to Retirement	Inflation Adjustment Factors		
	3%	4%	5%
5	1.159	1.217	1.276
10	1.344	1.480	1.629
20	1.806	2.191	2.653
30	2.427	3.243	4.322

SOURCE: American Society of CLU & ChFC

Suppose you're ten years from retirement and you expect inflation to increase 4 percent per year in the interim. Multiply the $37,000 gross income you'll need, in current dollars, by 1.480, the appropriate inflation adjustment factor. You'll wind up with $54,760. That's roughly the amount of gross income you'll need to maintain your current living standard in retirement.

Once you have this number, you can plan for making *sure* your retirement income will be adequate. You can, for example, expect to receive Social Security retirement benefits. Contact the Social Security Administration for an estimate of what your future benefits will be. Call 800-772-1213 for the appropriate form. You should check on your record every few years, since after three years you lose your right to correct errors.

In addition, either you or your employer may be contributing to a tax-deferred retirement plan on your behalf. Check with your company's benefits department, or a CPA, for an estimate of how much you can expect to receive in retirement.

The Dream Deferred

If you're relying on an employer's pension, take steps to make sure it will be there when you need it. At times, employers "borrow" from the plan and "forget" to repay the money. In other cases, they just steal it.

Consider the plight of James R., a shop foreman who worked for a small company in Irving, Texas, for twenty years. The owner of the company pleaded guilty to embezzling $103,000 from the employees' profit-sharing plans, including $33,000 that belonged to James—most of his life's savings. The employer convinced the judge that he was broke, so had to pay back only $100 per month. At that rate, it would take eighty-six years to reach $103,000. In the meantime, James had to forego retirement and find another job.

Such abuses can happen anywhere, but employees of small companies are particularly vulnerable because the authorities don't find it cost-effective to chase after every $103,000 swindle. You can't rely on someone else to watch over your nest egg; you have to do it yourself.

Your employer *must* supply you with a plan summary and annual reports. If you can't get these reports from your employer, or if you suspect you won't get the money you've been promised, write or call the Pension and Welfare Benefits Administration, Office of Program Services, Department of Labor, 200 Constitution Ave., N.W., Washington, DC 20210; 202-219-8776.

Increasingly, employers are terminating their pension plans, to avoid the regulatory burden and expense. If this happens to you, you're not necessarily wiped out: You likely will be entitled to a distribution of contributions already made on your behalf. You can find out by contacting the Pension Benefit Guaranty Corp., Participant Services Div., 1200 K St., N.W., Washington, DC 20005-4026; 202-326-4014. The Labor Department publishes "What You Should Know About Pension Law," available free from the U.S. Dept. of Labor, Division of Technical Assistance and Inquiries, 200 Constitution Avenue, N.W., Washington, DC 20216.

If you can't get satisfaction from these agencies, try the Pension Rights Center, 918 16th St., N.W., Suite 704, Washington, DC 20006-2902; 202-296-3776. This research group offers a booklet, "Where to Look for Help With a Pension Problem," for $8.50, that includes advice on how to proceed in cases of underfunding, mismanagement, and fraud. Another publication, "Protecting Your Pension Money," also is available.

Looking Out for Number One

Assuming you'll receive the full pension to which you're entitled, the total of your expected income from Social Security and retirement plans may still fall short of your retirement income needs. If so, it's up to you to make up the difference. Generally, that difference will come from a combination of earned income and investment income.

Say you expect to need $55,000 a year, in gross retirement income, with $30,000 per year likely from Social Security and retirement plans. You'd need another $25,000 a year, perhaps $10,000 from working part-time, and $15,000 a year in investment income.

Beyond Bonds

Once you know how much investment income you'll need in retirement, you can begin to accumulate an appropriate amount. A portfolio of $150,000–$200,000, for example, might be enough to generate the $15,000 per year in our example, depending on future interest rates.

The classic strategy for retirement investing is to concentrate on stocks while you're younger. As you get older, and thus closer to retirement, you then move into bonds, for higher income and less exposure to stock-market volatility. By the time you retire, you're fully invested in income-producing bonds.

Well—not *all* classics age gracefully. As mentioned, retirements last longer these days, and you've got to stay ahead of inflation to maintain purchasing power. You won't enjoy the inflation protection you'll need if your portfolio is *solely* in bonds and bond-type investments.

In the 1980s, retirees might have been able to justify loading up their portfolios with bonds. Interest rates were high enough so that double-digit yields were possible, with only moderate risk. In the mid-1990s, though, bonds were offering only modest returns. Therefore, you need to leaven your retirement portfolio with solid stocks for greater returns, so that your retirement will be comfortable, no matter how long you wind up living.

Stock Answers

In 1994, the Institute for Econometric Research (Fort Lauderdale, Florida) released one of the longest-term studies of investment returns ever attempted. It shows that from 1871 through 1993, common stocks gained 8.3 percent per year, after inflation. In other words, stocks have doubled every nine years, in real terms. If that doesn't impress you, consider that $1 invested in stocks in 1871 would have grown to nearly $18,000 by 1994.

By contrast, $1 invested in Treasury bills would have grown to $9, after inflation, and $1 in gold would have grown to $1.40 (that dollar would have lost ground, to 86 cents, if you assume a token storage and insurance fee). As the Institute points out, except for two 25 percent corrections (1929–33 and 1968–74), "Investors who bought stock at any time during the 123-year period—even at cyclical tops—made money if they simply held on for five or ten years."

If you're facing a lengthy retirement, put *at least half* of your money into stocks. Gold, T-bills, and money-market funds might preserve your principal, and bonds might beat inflation by a few points, but you need *stocks* in order to build wealth. Therefore, you should go into your retirement with a portfolio similar to the one you used to build a retirement fund, mixing stocks or stock funds with your bonds. As you grow older, you can shift from stocks to bonds. By the time you're in your eighties, your portfolio can be heavily weighted to income-producing vehicles.

Paltry Pensions

For some retirees, it's possible to put even more retirement money into stocks. They can turn down their longtime employer's pension, take the cash instead, and invest in stocks or stock funds.

Typically, when you retire you'll be offered an annuity from your employer. If you choose a *single-life annuity*, payments will continue until your death. If you opt for a *joint-and-survivor annuity*, the payments will continue for the lives of yourself and your spouse. Joint-and-survivor annuities provide lower monthly payments than single-life annuities, because the payments likely will go on for a longer time period. However, these annuities are based on current interest rates, which may lead to extremely low payout rates. In 1994, for example, employer-provided annuities typically assumed an investment return of only 5.1 percent.

Some employers will give you the option of taking a lump sum instead of a monthly pension. If you have the choice, take the lump sum and roll it into an Individual Retirement Account (IRA). The lower the assumed-interest rate, the higher the lump sum you'll receive.

When Lower Means Higher

Here's the reason for this seeming paradox. Say you're offered $1,000 per month, or $12,000 per year, from an employer annuity. If interest rates are high, that kind of an income may be possible with a lump sum of $100,000. But in a low-interest-rate environment you might need $150,000 to generate that $1,000 per month. So take your lump sum and roll it into an IRA. If you shop around among insurance companies, you'll likely find a much better deal on an annuity.

Take the example of George, age sixty-five, who's entitled to a $1,250 monthly pension. Using a 5.1 percent investment assumption, he'd be entitled to a $190,000 lump sum. With that parked in his IRA, George could easily get quotes from numerous insurance companies. *Kiplinger's Personal Finance* magazine has reported that every insurance company recently surveyed would pay more than $1,250 per month to a sixty-five-year-old with a $190,000 lump sum. Kansas City Life, a top-rated insurance company, offered 14 percent more— $1,430 per month. That's an extra $180 per month, or $2,160 per year, for one's entire retirement. To find the best deal on annuity payouts, you can buy a sample issue of *Annuity and Life Insurance Shopper* newsletter (800-872-6684) for $20.

While employers were paying out as if money earned 5.1 percent, insurers were basing payments on rates up to 6 percent. You can do still better if you hold on to your lump sum and invest on your own, mainly in stocks. If you earn 8 percent, say, you can pull out much more money, each and every year, than you can with an employer or an insurance-company annuity.

Spread Your Wealth

Whether you have an IRA rollover, an outside portfolio, or both, you can select your own stocks, as long as you diversify. Assuming an average $50 share price, you can buy a round lot of 100 shares for $5,000. You could invest in ten different issues for $50,000, and twenty issues for $100,000. For many retirees, that would be feasible, were they to receive a large distribution from an employer plan.

Just because you focus on stocks in your early retirement years, that doesn't mean you have to be reckless. If you emphasize blue-chip stocks, and especially those paying steady dividends, you can enjoy both income and growth potential.

Those blue-chip issues should be scattered among the key sectors of the economy: "Buy" a consumer-goods company, a high-tech company, a utility, an oil giant. Put some money into health care. Purchase a couple of multinationals. Besides your focus on proven, dividend-paying companies, grab some promising smaller companies, too.

If you're concerned about making stock-market commitments today, and your money is currently invested heavily in bonds, cash equivalents, and the like, you can use a *dollar-cost averaging approach* to move into the market: Each quarter, you can invest perhaps $10,000 or $20,000 in equities, until you have say $100,000 or $200,000 in stocks. By investing over an extended time period, you'll get the advantage of buying low, in case of a market downturn.

Feeling Mutual

If you'd rather not pick your own stocks, you can get professional management through mutual funds. Again, diversification is crucial— you'll want several funds rather than just one or two. You might as well buy *no-loads*, if *you're* going to do the work of researching and picking funds.

Morningstar, Inc., which tracks mutual-fund performance, has come up with an interesting approach to stock-fund diversification. If you buy, for example, a growth fund, an aggressive growth fund, a growth-and-income fund, and a small-cap fund, you may think you've diversified. However, you may have invested in four funds that all buy small companies, all using an earnings-growth approach to pick stocks.

If you select your funds based on top performance for the past few years, you may wind up with a bunch of small-growth stocks in the same industry—communications or financial services or whatever else has been hot recently. You're really not diversified, even if you own several funds holding hundreds of different companies. If one market sector suddenly goes out of favor, and many of your companies are in that sector, you could suffer a sizable loss of principal.

To avoid this problem, Morningstar has come up with "style boxes." In effect, these are grids showing which sizes of companies a fund holds (small, medium, or large), and what investment style it pursues (growth, value, or blend). By mixing style boxes, you can have a truly diversified mutual-fund portfolio.

Suppose, for example, you start out with Kaufmann Fund, a top-performing, aggressive growth fund. Its style box shows it's a small-cap fund looking for earnings growth.

For a growth fund, you might choose Crabbe Huson, another outstanding performer, with a style box that shows mid-cap stocks and a blended investment style. Round out your portfolio with Legg Mason Total Return Fund, a big-cap, value fund in the growth-and-income category. Once you have a foundation of three such funds in place, you can further diversify with a *sector fund, international fund, junk-bond fund*, and the like.

What if you don't want to make any decisions at all—no stockpicking, no mutual-fund selection? If your retirement fund is large enough (generally over $500,000 but sometimes as low as $100,000), you can ask your friends and relatives for references to a first-class stockbroker. Then, ask the broker to set you up in a *wrap account* with one or more money managers: with these accounts, you'll pay a stiff fee (usually 3 percent of assets under management) but you'll get professional management without having to worry about churning, because that 3 percent covers all fees, including brokers' commissions.

Whichever path you choose, be reasonable in your expectations. Remember, stocks have grown by around 8 percent per year, after inflation. With inflation running around 3 percent in the mid-1990s, you could expect to earn about 11 percent in stocks, including dividends.

So be skeptical about anyone who *promises* you 20 percent or 30 percent per year. That just can't be done—there's not enough money around. As the Institute for Econometric Research points out, if you had invested $1 in 1871 and earned 30 percent per year, you'd have $103 trillion—more than the Gross National Product of the entire world!

SUMMING UP

• As people retire earlier and live longer, it becomes vital for retirees to stretch out their retirement funds.

• In general, you'll need a retirement income that's around 70 percent of your preretirement income; and that retirement income should grow to keep pace with inflation.

• You can't enjoy growth and inflation protection if your retirement money is invested heavily in bonds, CDs, etc. Instead, you should invest most of your retirement funds in stocks, which have far outperformed bonds over virtually every time period.

• If you pick your own stocks, be sure to diversify among proven companies in a variety of industries.

• Rather than pick individual stocks, you can invest in mutual funds, as long as you make certain that your funds hold different types of companies and pursue different investment strategies.

• With a "wrap" account, your broker arranges for a money manager to handle your portfolio, in return for a flat fee that covers all expenses.

20

Let the Sun Shine In

In Retirement, Avoid Real-Estate Ripoffs and Ravening Tax Men

Most people see a "retirement dream-home" of their own at the end of the rainbow. Yours might well be located in a resort area, though perhaps a convenient urban one would be more practicable. Wherever you hope to wind up, your dream could turn into a nightmare if you choose the wrong kind of residence at the wrong time.

Take the case of Steve and Meg L., who moved from New York to Florida and quickly purchased a new home there. A year later, Steve had a stroke and was admitted to a nursing home for a long stay. Their income was squeezed, yet they couldn't sell their house to get at their capital, because of a weak housing market.

Or, consider what happened to Richard and Judy S., who moved from Milwaukee to Phoenix, where they bought a condo apartment. Unfortunately, the building sponsors weren't able to sell enough apartments, so they allowed the property to fall into disrepair. Now

Richard and Judy live in a building with failing services and virtually no hope to sell at a reasonable price.

To avoid such disasters, you need to be methodical and not let your emotions overwhelm your common sense. For example, *don't* buy a retirement home just because of a glossy sales brochure or a slick sales pitch. Instead, start out with a list of expectations—all the things you're *really* looking for in the place. Then search until you find a home that will satisfy as many of these preconditions as it will take to sell itself to you.

First Things First

Your first step should be to decide *where* you'd like to live in retirement, basing your choice on at least some of the following criteria:

• Are there family members—your children, perhaps—there whom you'd like to live near? (Or those whom you'd like to avoid?)

• If you've lived in or near a major metropolitan area all your life, you may not be ready to live out your life in a rural or semirural area. Conversely, if you have spent your life in a small town, you may not feel comfortable in Greater Phoenix or Miami.

• Unless you're a dedicated skier, you probably envision a retirement home free of overcoats and heating bills. But there's a continent's worth of difference between Florida's humidity and Arizona's blazing but dry heat. In fact, there's a huge difference between Florida's Keys, in the tropics, and the more moderate temperatures in the Panhandle region.

Your health might dictate an arid climate rather than a wet one. Also, don't forget allergies, if you have any. And if hay fever ruins your summers, choose a new location carefully.

• Certain states tax heavily, some lightly. Among popular retirement destinations, Florida, Nevada, and Texas are among the states that have *no personal income tax.*

Before you move, check with your new home's Chamber of Commerce or tax department for a complete picture: property tax, sales tax, and estate tax, *as well as* income tax. In some areas of Florida, for example, property taxes have risen tenfold in the past twenty-five years. Don't walk into any tax surprises!

• You probably want a lower cost of living in retirement. A couple who had been living in an $80,000 condo in New York City's outer boroughs recently bought a house of the same size in Delray Beach, Florida, for $40,000. Living on their Social Security and pension income of $24,000, this couple saved $5,000 per year in taxes, housing, heating, and clothing costs, compared to what they had been paying in New York.

Another couple living in a $300,000 home in New Jersey bought a smaller but still sizable home in Sarasota, Florida for under $100,000. With total income over $100,000 from Social Security, pensions, and investments, this couple wound up saving nearly $20,000 per year. You too can find retirement areas where you'll be able to live well for less money.

In general, the farther you get from large metropolitan areas and prime tourist spots, the lower your living costs will be. If you want to rent a one-bedroom apartment near Honolulu, for example, you'd pay over $1,000 per month, on average. In the next-most-expensive areas—San Francisco, Washington, D.C., New York City, Boston— apartment rents were over $700 per month, as of last report, while they topped $600 in metro Los Angeles and Chicago. These were *averages* for suburban apartments. You'll pay much more to live in a prime neighborhood in the city itself.

If you're content to retire in a small-town setting, you'll slash your living costs dramatically. Areas such as Corbin (Kentucky), Newport (Tennessee), Hennessey (Oklahoma), Scottsboro (Alabama), and Casper (Wyoming) offer one-bedroom apartments renting for $250 or less per month.

• Safety counts, too. There's nowhere you can go to avoid crime altogether these days, but some areas are safer than others. Again, urban and suburban areas tend to have more violent crime and more theft than do small towns.

• In social services, the reverse is true. If you need access to a particular type of service, you're more likely to find it in a metropolitan area. State and local agencies on aging may offer special programs for seniors.

• Health care is vital to most retirees, especially older ones. Make sure that proper health- and medical care will be available before you move.

Inspect local health facilities, and talk to residents about their doctors. The American Hospital Association publishes an annual "Guide to the Health Care Field" with state-by-state listings of every hospital in America, including specialties. Check into medical costs, too. Florida, for example, has surprisingly high health-care costs: A. Foster Higgins, a benefits consulting firm, found medical bills more than 50 percent higher in Florida than in New Jersey!

Get your health insurance and Medicare supplemental insurance lined up before you move, *especially* to Florida. Some insurers in other states will permit you to retain coverage even after you move to Florida—where premiums would be higher.

Little Things Mean a Lot

The factors listed above will be of prime importance to most retirees. However, after you feel comfortable with the major points, you can turn to seemingly minor considerations that can add up to a big difference in your retirement life style.

If access to cultural events is important to you, look into the entertainment offerings before relocating. Are there community theaters, dinner theaters, or major stage productions in the area? Will you find museums, ballet, opera, symphonies? Is there much night life? (You'll probably want convenient restaurants, movie theaters, and video-rental stores, too.)

You may choose a retirement setting because it permits you to pursue a favored activity, such as sailing, skiing, or golf. Or, you might pick a new home because you'll have access to big-league baseball, football, or whatever.

Many housing developments and apartment complexes offer exercise centers with pools, bicycle-type exercise machines, and classes in water aerobics or aerobic dancing. You'll also want to see if the area offers places for walking, especially if you walk regularly for exercise.

What will you do with your spare time in retirement? In Manhattan's Greenwich Village, you can take books out of a library, walk homeless dogs at a shelter, join political organizations, attend college courses, and so on (and on). In a small town, there might not be nearly as much to occupy your days and nights.

You may want to live near people your own age, who are more likely than others to share your interests. When you're surrounded by younger people with children, you may not have much in common with your neighbors anymore. You also may want to live in a certain ethnic neighborhood, or in an otherwise diversified community.

News Worthy

How do you find out about all the factors mentioned above—crime, sports, cost of living, etc?

One way to begin is by picking out a few areas where you might like to retire. Three or four cities on Florida's Gulf Coast, for example. Then, take out a subscription to the local newspapers in each city. There's no better way to get a feel for local issues. Too, *Editor and Publisher's International Yearbook*, which lists every newspaper in the United States, is available at most libraries. And many newspapers offer short-term subscriptions, mailing to your hometown.

Read these local papers with a particular eye to the police reports and crime stories. If a household robbery is big news, the community probably has a low crime rate. You'll also want to see if any new taxes have been proposed, whether residents are complaining about increased traffic congestion, and so on.

Pounding the Pavement

Reading newspaper articles about possible locations is a good way to begin, but *nothing* beats a visit to the area. To get this firsthand experience, take a vacation, or rent, in the vicinity before deciding on making a permanent move. When you're there, you can have face-to-face conversations with local police officers, storekeepers, and potential neighbors. You'll thereby learn what the newspapers *don't* cover.

While you're in town, call some local physicians, to get an idea of how much an office visit will cost. In fact, find out if local physicians *will* accept new Medicare patients. With Medicare fees capped, some physicians *won't* take on more seniors.

Ask some local residents who have moved from other areas how hard it is to get a driver's license. Some states require waiting periods for all new residents, but others have separate requirements for drivers over sixty-five, including more frequent driver tests and medical or vision exams.

Check into public transportation, too, to see if you can live comfortably in the neighborhood without a car. As you grow older, you may want to drive less—or even give up your car altogether. Strong bus service is a plus. Also, find out if cabs or car services are available (and reliable).

To get answers to all your questions, talk to people you meet at the post office, the gas station, the supermarket. Their personal experiences will more than likely be far more valuable than anything you read in brochures from the Chamber of Commerce or the Convention Bureau.

For a better look at how everyday life is for the average resident, do the everyday things. Visit the library to see what sort of books it carries. See how much variety there is among local restaurants, prices on their menus, and the hours they stay open. Find out whether or not stores stay open on Sunday.

If you're actively religious, check your choice of the local houses of worship there, to see which you'll be comfortable with. Attend both a service and a church function, to find out how you might relate to that congregation. Take with you a grocery receipt from home, so you can compare prices while you're away. You'll get a cook's-eye look (instead of a cockeyed one) at the nitty-grittiest cost of living in those prospective communities.

Patience Pays Off

After you've done your research and your on-site visits, you probably will have quite a good idea of where you'd like to live in retirement. One or another place will particularly appeal to you, for either tangible or intangible reasons—or both. Picking a city or town where you'd like to live is half the battle in choosing a retirement home.

There's *another* half, though: picking a specific house. You need to be absolutely certain you're getting value for your money. (In our next chapter, we'll have advice on choosing a retirement *community*. For now, we'll assume that you'll be living independently, outside of a *planned* development.) The best way to avoid a bad housing buy is not to buy at all! Instead, *rent* a house—or an apartment. At least, that's how you should dip your toe into any local housing market.

There are a few advantages to this approach. First, you preserve your capital: In case you need money for an emergency, you have it handy. (After you put your money into a house, it may not be easy to get it out, via either a sale *or* a loan.)

Second, no matter *how* much research you do, there's *no* way to really know a local housing market without living there for a time. If you *rent* for a while, you'll see what your expenses are, and know specifically where you want to live. You'll be able to make a savvier choice on the rent-versus-buy issue.

Shelter Plus Upside

Are there advantages to buying? Certainly. If you buy for all-cash, or with a fixed-rate mortgage, you lock in the purchase price. You won't have to worry about rents increasing, over ten or twenty years or longer. You may enjoy long-term appreciation, as well.

There also may be tax advantages to buying rather than renting. When you sell a house and move to a new area in retirement, a large capital gain may be triggered. By buying a retirement home, you may be able to defer the tax, or at least reduce it.

(Note, however, that homeowners over age 55 are entitled to a one-time tax exclusion of $125,000 worth of capital gains on the sale of a principal residence. Only if you have a larger gain will you need to pay tax. Thus, not every retiree will have to buy a retirement home in order to trim taxes on capital gains.)

In addition, buying a house may provide ongoing tax advantages. Property taxes and mortgage interest are deductible, whereas rent is not. Again, note that many people are in a lower tax bracket after retirement. The lower your tax bracket, the less valuable your tax deductions, including those for property taxes and mortgage interest.

So, buying a retirement home may offer tax benefits *and* the chance for appreciation. On the other hand, owning a house may mean more expense *and* responsibilities. Thus, many retirees prefer condo apartments, where one condo fee covers many of those expenses and responsibilities. Some housing developments, too, allow homeowners to pay a fee to cover upkeep of common areas.

Weigh all the alternatives before deciding to buy. Often, you'll be able to rent a house or condo with an *option* to buy. Even if you *need* to buy a house, to maintain tax deferral, you'll have two years to make a decision, after the sale of your prior residence.

The more you shop around, the more likely you'll avoid overpaying for a house, or buying a lemon. Pay a price that's comparable to real-estate transactions you see reported in the local newspaper, or to the price you hear about from friends and acquaintances. Hire an independent inspector to evaluate *any* house before you buy. If you're considering a condo project or a housing development, get financial statements and show them to a CPA of your choosing: You don't want to buy into a distressed project.

In short, don't rush into buying a retirement home. Move along carefully, consulting regularly with relatives and acquaintances you trust. It's much easier to make a mistake than to unmake one!

When You Move, Move

Some retirees like the idea of "doubling up." And why not? It's a great deal, if you can afford it. Half the year, you're in New York (for example), enjoying all the summertime cultural facilities. Then, when the weather turns cold, "snowbirds" head for Florida, where the livin' is easier.

But dual residency *can* be a tax trap: You don't want to pay *two* income taxes and *two* estate taxes. Therefore, take all steps necessary to establish what the lawyers call *domicile*, preferably in the lower-tax state.

How can you establish a domicile in, say, Florida rather than New York?

- Move your bank accounts.
- Change your auto registration.
- Change your driver's license.
- Establish relationships with a doctor, lawyer, accountant, and broker.
- Join a house of worship.
- Change your voter's registration.
- Pay your federal income tax from your Florida address.
- Change your address on all legal documents, including your passport.
- Write a new will.
- Perhaps most important, be sure you spend more time in Florida than in New York each year.

SUMMING UP

- When you choose a retirement home, you should do so methodically rather than emotionally.
- Start by choosing an area where you'd like to live in retirement—because of family relationships, low costs, or recreational opportunities—or some combination.
- Narrow your choice to specific communities by subscribing to local newspapers, making site visits, and talking to local residents.

• After you have selected a city or town, rent there *before* considering buying a house, so you won't tie up your capital.

• You may decide to buy, rather than rent, in order to prolong a tax deferral or to participate in housing appreciation.

• If you decide to buy, check carefully into the physical and fiscal condition of the development before making a commitment.

• After you make a retirement move to a low-tax state, take all steps necessary to sever your relationship with your old, high-tax state.

21

Community Sense

Pick a Retirement Development Without Getting Your Pocket Picked

As America has aged and the over-sixty-five population has expanded, the real-estate industry has been quick to address this growing market. Many *retirement communities* have been created, designed specifically to serve senior citizens. The variety is enormous, in amenities as well as in financial arrangements. Therefore, don't make a commitment to a retirement community until you've evaluated several alternatives.

When you first retire, relatively young and in reasonably good health, you'll probably want a community where you can live independently—in a house or an apartment. In a retirement community, you'll likely find yourself surrounded with neighbors who have common interests. Young married couples with children probably won't be around. Also, such a setting may offer you certain services that you wouldn't find in a standard apartment building or housing development. Start your search for the ideal community by looking at the

147

criteria mentioned previously: You'll want to live in a desirable location, in a physically sound home, among elements in solid financial condition.

But there are *other* factors you should look for in a retirement community. Perhaps most of all, you'll want to know about the people who live there. A "community" should be more than just a housing project with a lot of old residents. It should be the place where you look forward to spending much of your later life. You should if possible have close friends there, people you like to be around. On the down side, if you find yourself in a community with people you *don't* like, or with whom you have little in common, your retirement likely will not be very pleasant.

So visit a retirement community before making it your permanent residence (you may be able to rent there for a while). Look at the people already living there. If you and your spouse are in your early sixties, eager to play tennis and golf, you're not likely to be happy in a community where everyone else seems much older and generally infirm. On the other hand, you may be encouraged if you visit a community where everybody is zipping by on roller skates and bikes.

Be honest with yourself. If you feel most comfortable living among people of a certain ethnic or religious background, *make sure* that's who you'll find there.

Other features of a retirement community may influence your decision. You'll probably want good security, for example. And activities are important, too: Whether your passion is fishing or bridge or amateur theater, you'll want to be sure you can pursue it. (The same goes for your spouse.) You also may appreciate a retirement community that offers architecture that's pleasing to the eye, in a beautiful natural setting.

Cream of the Crop

In 1993, *New Choices* magazine picked the twenty top retirement communities in the United States, all of which accept residents without regard to race or religion but which have a minimum age requirement—generally around age fifty-five:

- Bayview Village at Port Ludlow, Washington; 800-872-1323.
- Bradford Village, Santee, South Carolina; 800-331-1457.

• The Fairways at Leisure World, Silver Spring, Maryland; 301-598-2100.

• Green Valley, in Green Valley, Arizona; 602-625-7575.

• The Harbours at Aberdeen Golf & Country Club, Boynton Beach, Florida; 800-749-9697.

• Heritage Village, Southbury, Connecticut; 203-264-7570.

• The Lakes at Gig Harbor, in Gig Harbor, Washington; 800-822-8875.

• Leisure Village Ocean Hills, Oceanside, California; 619-758-7080.

• The Maples at Old Country Road, Wenham, Massachusetts; 508-468-4950.

• Oakmont, Santa Rosa, California; 707-539-1530.

• Sonata Bay Club, Bayville, New Jersey; 800-952-9521.

• Sun City, Bermuda Dunes, California; 800-533-5932.

• Sun City, Las Vegas, Nevada; 800-843-4848.

• Sun City Center, in Sun City Center, Florida; 800-237-8200.

• Sun Lakes Country Club, Banning, California; 800-368-8887.

• Sun Lakes Country Clubs, Sun Lakes, Arizona; 800-321-8643.

• Swansgate, Greenville, South Carolina; 803-233-1107.

• The Villages Golf and Country Club, San Jose, California; 408-274-4400.

• Westbrook Village, Peoria, Arizona; 800-892-2838.

• Woodlake Village, Myrtle Beach, South Carolina; 800-651-0020.

Some of the standout communities are intimate: The Maples has only fifty-five co-op units in eight buildings, set on eight acres. At the other end of the spectrum, Green Valley has a mix of 10,000 housing units—apartments, attached clusters, townhouses, single-family houses—spread over 5,000 acres.

Amenities vary, too. The Villages Golf and Country Club, for example, has a 550-acre nature preserve, teeming with red foxes and wild turkeys. Florida's Sun City Center offers 126 holes of golf (seven eighteen-hole courses). The Fairways at Leisure World, near Washington, D.C., is frequently visited by current and former federal officials, while Heritage Village offers lectures by professors from three nearby universities. Depending on your interests, you may find your ideal retirement home in one of these places, or in some other community.

To find out which community is best for *you*, firsthand visits are necessary. Many communities offer short-term or seasonal rentals in unsold units. Or, you may be able to house-sit for a resident who's on vacation.

Only by living in a community will you learn what it's *really* like. Therefore, you're probably better off *not* moving into a startup retirement community. Wait until it's up and running, so you can see what you'd be getting into.

Money Matters

Although some of the retirement communities on the list offer rental apartments, most consist mainly of houses and condos for sale. Prices are literally all over the lot. Bradford Village is the least-expensive community on the list, with houses starting as low as $78,500, according to *New Choices*, while The Lakes at Gig Harbor includes only manufactured homes, selling in the $83,000–$105,000 range.

On the other hand, three of the California communities (Oakmont, The Villages, Leisure Village Ocean Hills) have *no* homes selling for *less* than $209,000, and going as high as $389,000 at Oakmont. Green Valley is so huge that it has houses in *all* price categories, ranging as high as $500,000.

If you're going to buy a house or condo in a retirement community, exercise normal real-estate prudence. Shop around so you don't overpay. And find out if there's an active resale market, so you'll be able to get your money out if you decide to move.

In Good Hands

Retirement communities such as those mentioned above appeal chiefly to younger, more-active retirees. But there's another type of retirement community, one aimed at older people, that is growing in popularity. With these developments—often known as *continuing care communities*—you may have to pay a huge up-front fee, so you need to be extremely cautious.

Take the case of William and Marilou M., who built a chain of pastry shops in Tulsa. In the 1970s, they took early retirement, sold their business, and purchased a house in Lake Placid, Florida. Twenty years later, at ages eighty and seventy-five, they sold their house, taking a $45,000 loss in a weak real-estate market. Then they paid a nonrefundable $276,000 "entrance fee" to live in a three-bedroom apartment. Plus, they agreed to pay an additional $3,000 per month as an ongoing fee.

What was the attraction? The apartment complex offers many amenities, from golf to local transportation. They're entitled to one meal per day in the main dining room. Perhaps most important, if either William or Marilou (or both) would have to go into a nursing home, there is one on the grounds—at no extra cost. And the other spouse may stay in their apartment. Thus, they're effectively buying catastrophic insurance as well as a place to live.

Price Points

Over 400,000 Americans lived in about 1,000 such continuing-care communities in 1993, up from 170,000 in 1983. Also known as *life-care communities*, they're especially attractive to retirees seventy-five and older, who may have concerns about their health. Residents may be in excellent health, as William and Marilou were. If residents are not quite as healthy, they may be able to live independently if they have *some* personal care, which is what these facilities provide. Or they may decline to the point where they need to live in a nursing home. (Some "assisted living facilities" are heavier on the care, lighter on the recreational facilities for active retirees.)

Today, with nursing-home costs anywhere from $30,000 to $100,000 per year, a long-term stay can impoverish a family and beggar the spouse who continues to live at home. Thus, continuing-care communities have enormous appeal.

They often have enormous costs, too. Entrance fees may be less than $100,000 but may reach $400,000. A complex with a low entrance fee may compensate with a high monthly fee, ranging up to $3,500 per person ($7,000 per couple). Fees may be based on age and health: Younger people may pay a higher entrance fee, while healthy people may have a lower monthly bill.

If the entrance fee is nonrefundable, a portion (usually 20 percent to 30 percent) may be tax-deductible as a prepayment of future health care. The healthier you are, and the more likely you are to outlive your life expectancy, the more attractive a nonrefundable entrance fee will be. They're based on age, so chances are that you'll get more housing for your money. However, paying an entrance fee *isn't* the same as buying a house. If you're deferring a gain from selling a principal residence, paying an entrance fee will trigger the tax, rather than maintain the deferral.

Money-Back Guarantees

Newer communities, particularly those established since 1985, offer partial refunds on entrance fees. Anywhere from 75 percent to 90 percent of the entrance fee will be returned, should you decide to move. Upon your death (or the death of your surviving spouse), the refund will go to your heirs. Thus, you're not locked into one community, and you will leave a larger inheritance.

There's a down side to refundable fees, though. They're often 10 percent to 25 percent higher than nonrefundable fees at comparable facilities. Also, there's a tax headache.

The IRS treats the refundable portion of the fee as a loan, and taxes you on the "interest" you don't actually receive. Say you pay a $200,000 entrance fee that's 90 percent refundable. That would be considered a $180,000 loan from you to the retirement community. Even though the community isn't paying you interest, the IRS will "impute" interest to you. At a 5 percent rate, for example, you'd have $9,000 in "phantom income" per year, on which you'd owe income tax.

So get all the facts before you spend $100,000, $200,000, or more on a retirement-community entrance fee. Read over the contract thoroughly. Consult with your lawyer *and* your CPA. Not only do you want to know all the financial and tax ramifications, but also, you want to know that the project is fiscally sound, before putting up your life's savings. If the complex goes under, you may find yourself without *any* money or *any* services, just when they're sorely needed.

Club Dues

Not all continuing-care communities demand huge up-front fees. Some are membership clubs: You buy a membership, which either you or your estate can sell.

This approach has risks. What happens if your membership brings a lower resale price, or if it can't be sold at all? Also, memberships generally cost 25 percent to 50 percent more than a nonrefundable entrance fee.

In other developments, apartments are sold as cooperatives or condos. Here, capital-gains deferral can be maintained. However, prices may be high, and owners bear resale risk. Also, if you've already taken the $125,000 capital-gains exclusion for home sellers over age fifty-five, the capital-gains deferral won't be meaningful.

Again, check carefully into the terms of the contract, and also into the financial health of the project, before making any major decisions. You might prefer a community with no entrance fees at all, paying monthly fees that depend on the level of services you require, and protecting yourself against long nursing-home stays by buying long-term care insurance (see Chapter 17).

Crunch the Numbers

Be wary of new developments, especially if the developer lacks a track record. For established projects, occupancy rates are crucial. If a community is less than 80 percent occupied and it's more than two years old, that may be a warning sign.

Always ask to see a community's most recent audited financial statement, which should be available from the management upon request. You (or a financial adviser) can check to see if the project is meeting its debt service and operating costs while maintaining sufficient reserves for emergencies. In some developments ski, golf, or tennis facilities are owned by a partnership of homeowners. If that's the case, you can request copies of federally mandated property reports, and other financial documents, to help you judge the project's financial health.

In addition, check the county clerk's office to see if liens have been filed against the property for nonpayment of taxes or secured debt. Also check with the local Better Business Bureau, to ascertain whether complaints have been made against the property.

The American Association of Retired Persons (AARP) has identified six "red flags" that can warn of potential trouble in a retirement community:

1. *Overbuilding.* There may be too many retirement facilities for the local population to support.

2. *Low value.* Seemingly low prices may indicate that the buildings are poorly designed, while services will be subpar.

3. *Overborrowing.* If the developer spent too much money on the project, mainly with borrowed money, the project's revenues might not cover the interest payments.

4. *Insufficient and depleted financial reserves.* Real-estate projects need a "rainy day" fund.

5. *Poor marketing.* Units may have been sold by inexperienced or uninformed sales staff using an inappropriate marketing strategy.

6. *Financial and operational mismanagement.* The owners may be using current income for misguided expansion.

These red flags may overlap. If occupancy is low, revenues will be below projections and the project will not provide the amenities that residents expect. Then, some residents may move out, making the problems even worse. Your best strategy is to look for troubles before you decide to buy, so you can avoid them altogether.

SUMMING UP

- Younger, more-active retirees may prefer to live in a community that offers a wide range of recreational and social opportunities.
- Besides the services that are available, evaluate the people who might be your neighbors, before deciding upon a retirement community.
- Topflight retirement communities come in all price ranges, in all areas of the United States, so shop carefully before buying.
- Retirees in poor health and those over age seventy-five may prefer an assisted-living or continuing-care community offering food, housekeeping, and nursing-home services, if necessary.
- Many of these communities charge a large up-front fee (which may however be nonrefundable), no matter how short your stay as a resident in the complex.
- Other communities have refundable fees, but they're often higher than nonrefundable fees—and they generate tax problems.
- *Don't* make a large initial outlay to get into a retirement community without first learning all the details and comparing the cost to a straight rental plus purchase of a long-term-care insurance policy.
- Be wary of new developments, and those that are less than 80 percent occupied after two years of operation.

22

Avoid Publicity as Well as Probate

Living Trusts Lead to Quiet Asset Transfers

Dr. John D., ninety-one years old, still practices medicine. He's a little hard of hearing, but most of his patients continue to come to him anyway. They all tell him the same sort of thing, and he just nods his head.

This may seem amusing—but some aspects of Dr. John's advancing age aren't so funny. He has misplaced $700,000 worth of bonds, for example. They were registered (rather than bearer) bonds, but it cost a significant amount to get them reissued. In addition, the doctor wasn't keeping track of dividend or interest income, so his income-tax records were a shambles.

Unfortunately, this story is not all that unusual. As America ages, more of us will fall prey to Alzheimer's disease and other forms of senility. You may not want to admit it, but the time may come when you're elderly, retired, the possessor of extensive assets you've accumulated all your life—and unable to exercise rational control over those assets.

In such circumstances, both your wealth and your family's wealth may be at risk. Who'll sign your Social Security or pension checks? Who'll sell your securities or real estate? Who'll handle all the financial arrangements necessary to settle you into a nursing home?

Filling the Void

Unless the right steps are taken, *nobody* can do *anything* with an incompetent's assets. Someone—usually a spouse or a grown child— must apply to a court, in order to be named guardian. Only after the spending of a couple of thousand dollars on lawyer's fees and court costs (and after waiting until the court can schedule a hearing) can the guardian take over.

There's an even darker side to guardianship. As you get older, and perhaps frailer, *anyone* can petition the court to be named your guardian (sometimes called a *conservator*). If this does happen, *you* will get a written notice of a hearing. To object, you'll have to hire a lawyer and try to prove, in court, that you're in fact quite competent, thank you. The prospective guardian might then bring in friends or neighbors, however, to tell tales of seeing you walking around in your underwear, muttering to yourself—and so on.

What if you lose? You become a ward of the person who brought the petition! Indeed, in some jurisdictions you won't be able to do *anything* without the permission of your guardian.

In some states, it's relatively easy to become a guardian, even if the prospective ward protests. The subject's presence at the hearing may not even be required; medical proof of incompetence may not be at all necessary. To top it all off, a typical guardianship hearing lasts less than fifteen minutes—hardly enough time to convincingly demonstrate your lucidity, given your upset condition. And then afterward, it's extremely difficult to get a guardian removed.

On paper, guardians are required to operate under the supervision of a court. They're supposed to notify the court about what they're doing, and get permission for major expenditures. However, many probate courts (they're the ones that usually handle guardianships) have huge workloads, so judges often pay little attention to what guardians are doing. Therefore, if you receive a notice of a guardianship hearing, call a lawyer immediately. Hire one with some decent amount of experience in guardianship hearings. And ask your doctor or your accountant for references, if necessary.

Moreover, you should act *now*, while you're still competent, to avert future disaster. Even if you're a long way from your declining years, your *parents* may have assets you'd like to protect, for your sake as well as theirs. Their life's savings can be squandered, or lost to unscrupulous predators, if they reach the point where they no longer can manage their own affairs.

Put Your Trust in Living Trusts

Perhaps the best way to avoid such a disaster personally is to set up a trust while you're still in control of your faculties. Trusts aren't just for the Rockefellers and the DuPonts. If you have accumulated *any* meaningful wealth, trusts can help you to leave your property to your family with a minimum of trouble and expense.

A *trust* is a legal fiction created to own property. Virtually any attorney can set up a trust for you, but you should work with one who's experienced in this area, and preferably a member of the American College of Trust and Estate Counsel. For simple trusts, start-up costs should be relatively low—generally under $1,000.

A trust you create while you're still alive is called a *living trust*. One popular type is the *revocable* trust, which you can annul whenever you'd like. You, the creator of the trust, can act as the trustee who manages the trust funds, as well as the beneficiary who receives distributions from the trust. Therefore, you can transfer assets into a *revocable living trust*, keep control, and enjoy the income. You can sell assets from your trust, if you wish, and add new ones.

You'll probably want to transfer only a few assets into the trust at first, to hold down the cost and the paperwork. When you reach fifty-five or sixty (the age when health problems may become noticeable), selected assets can be transferred. The assets you transfer to the trust should be ones you'd want help in managing in case of incompetency, and ones that will be subject to probate after your death. Jointly owned property *shouldn't* go into a living trust.

Successor Stories

After you transfer assets into a trust, those assets no longer are owned by you, personally. If you become incapacitated, your chosen *successor trustee* can take control of those assets. Then there's continuity of management, so you won't have to worry about a family business, or investment property, or securities portfolio, being tied up in red tape.

With a living trust in place, you won't have to fear that a court will appoint a guardian or conservator in the event of disability or incompetence; control can be transferred in private, without any publicity. You can avoid the spectacle that surrounded Groucho Marx after he became incompetent and his family fought over his property.

There are two ways to plan for a change of control in case you do become incompetent: You can name your eventual successor as *co-trustee*, right from the beginning, or you can name what we've already identified as a successor trustee, to take over when necessary. Most people prefer to use a successor trustee. They thus control the trust assets without having to share power.

However, this all means that a specific action is necessary in order to change trustees. Most of the time, an incompetent person won't become obviously deranged overnight. Instead, from time to time he or she will begin to act irrationally. Who's to say where incompetence begins? Sometimes incompetence has to be certified by the family doctor, and at other times yet another doctor has to concur.

If you have absolute confidence in a spouse or grown child, you can name him or her as cotrustee and smooth the transition, because no trigger event is necessary. This strategy is especially attractive to professionals, and to others who won't want a written judgment that they're incapable.

The same issues cover your retirement plan (including an IRA or a Keogh), which may be your greatest asset. Generally, retirement plans must be held in a separate trust, not in your revocable living trust. Again, you can name a younger person as a cotrustee or a successor trustee, depending on whether you're willing to relinquish total control while you're still capable.

Negate Probate

A living trust also will help your family avoid probate after your death. Your successor trustee can quickly distribute trust assets according to your wishes.

On the other hand, assets you own personally *have* to go through probate, with few exceptions (jointly owned property, insurance policies, and pension plans with beneficiaries you've named). Probate can cost as much as 7 percent of your estate, and the lawyers get paid first, before anything goes to your family members. In some states, probate can take as long as two years, effectively tying up your assets. What's more, the probate process is on the public record. Thus, if you want to keep your affairs private, use a living trust.

With a living trust, you can accomplish most of your wealth-transfer goals, using a will only for those few assets not in the trust. In fact, a living trust is better than a will if you own property in more than one state, because your heirs won't have to go through probate in each state. A trust is easier to modify than a will if you relocate, or if your circumstances change significantly.

There are disadvantages, though. Here are two: Revocable living trusts are *not* tax shelters—while you're alive, the trust's income will flow through to your personal tax return. Also upon your death, trust assets *will* be included in your taxable estate.

If you want tax savings, you'll have to use another type of living trust: an *irrevocable living trust*. As the name suggests, such trusts remove assets from your control, with no turning back. However, you *can* name a reliable family member, friend, or financial adviser as trustee, and you *can* establish guidelines for the use of trust funds.

Whichever type of living trust you choose, you must take care to follow up. Assets must be retitled—from *your* name to the name of the trust. Otherwise, you and your family might not enjoy the benefits of protection, privacy, and probate avoidance.

SUMMING UP

• Some people will become incompetent as they grow older, jeopardizing their assets.

• You can protect your assets by putting them into a trust.

• A trust you set up while you're alive is called a *living trust.*

• A *revocable living trust,* which can be annulled, is useful for transferring assets without a guardianship hearing and for avoiding probate after your death.

• To provide tax shelter, a living trust *must* be irrevocable, which means you give up control over the trust assets.

• Assets must be retitled to the trust, if you are to receive full benefits from it.

23

Power Plays

Create an Impenetrable Paper
Barrier Against Incompetency

Living trusts provide excellent protection against incompetency, yet they have their shortcomings. For example, you won't be able to re-title all of your assets to trust ownership, and some assets you won't want to hold in trust. Therefore, a living trust can be supplemented by a *power of attorney*, a legal document that permits another party to act on your behalf. This document can cover assets *not* held in trust—such as automobiles or a checking account.

Even if you're not ready to title your assets to a living trust, a power of attorney can be invaluable. Dan M., for example, had a stroke while he was in his fifties, with no prior warning signals. He thereafter couldn't sign his name, a handicap which might have had serious financial consequences. Fortunately, however, he had executed a power of attorney—thus his son could sign checks and pay for private-duty nursing.

People with assets to protect should assign a power of attorney. In

160

doing so, you can even name more than one party, specifying whether they can act singly or must act in concert. For example, you might nominate both of your children as *attorneys-in-fact*, stating that they must be in agreement in order to act on your behalf. Naturally, any person or persons you name must be from among those you trust fully. This usually means at least one close—and younger—family member.

General powers of attorney, though, terminate when the person whose assets are at stake (the *principal*) becomes incompetent. Therefore, you should use a *durable* power of attorney, a variation recognized by all fifty states. Such powers will contain language along the lines of, "This power of attorney shall not be terminated by the principal's disability or incompetence." You can change or cancel a power of attorney at any time. (At your death, a durable power will automatically be cancelled.)

If you wish, you can assign different attorneys-in-fact responsibilities to different people. You may name your spouse to make your housing decisions, for example, and your son to manage all your financial affairs.

A Touch of Spring

Understandably, you may not want to give power over your assets to a family member while you're still in command of your faculties. Fortunately, *springing* powers of attorney are recognized in about twenty states, including California and New York. These powers won't "spring" (become effective) until specified events take place, such as incompetency—certified by a doctor—or entry into a nursing home.

What if your state doesn't recognize springing powers? You often can achieve the same result with a durable power accompanied by a letter stating that the springing power will go into effect *if* certain events take place. An attorney should hold both documents until they're needed.

When you're ready to execute a power of attorney, retain a lawyer who's experienced in *estate planning*. Such a lawyer likely will spell out the powers that the agreement conveys: managing property, making gifts, establishing trusts, filing tax returns, making retirement-plan elections, and so on. You might want to restrict possible gift recipients (e.g., to family members) and limit such gifts to the $10,000 annual gift-tax exemption.

Some financial institutions require the use of their own power-of-attorney forms. Check with your banks, brokers, and such, after a power of attorney has been drawn up. Send a copy to *each* institution, asking if there's any problem with the form.

Just because you execute a durable power of attorney, *don't* ignore the need for a living trust also. Some banks and brokerage firms that balk at accepting powers of attorney won't have any problems dealing with a successor trustee. Revocable living trusts also may be better than powers of attorney for people with extensive assets spread over more than one state.

Why not just give assets to your children, or put them in a joint account? Joint ownership works, in some circumstances—but you need to be careful about gift taxes. Also, holding assets in joint ownership may rob you of flexibility when it comes to estate planning, because the property automatically passes to the other owner at your death! Gifts are fine, as part of an estate plan, but you probably need a power of attorney, too.

Once Is Not Enough

After you execute a power of attorney, you should update it every year or two, a move which will increase the likelihood that your power will be honored. Otherwise, a challenger with an adverse interest may claim that it's invalid. Each time it's renewed, have *several* original powers of attorney executed and notarized, because some institutions will insist upon keeping one of these in their files.

Expect to pay a lawyer $1,000–$1,500 to create a power of attorney in the first place; renewing it shouldn't cost more than a token fee. To hold down the costs, make your decisions *before* you consult with a lawyer. If you tell the attorney which assets you want managed, and what specific instructions you'd like to include, you'll reduce appreciably the hours for which you'll be billed.

Parent Protection

Even if you think you're years away from incompetency, you may have to worry about your parents—or your spouse's parents. If either set loses their ability to manage their affairs, assets could be misplaced or stolen. Many scam artists prey on the elderly, and you could wind up not only without an inheritance, but also supporting your elderly parents or in-laws.

To help protect your entire family, go over your parents' financial affairs. Check to see that they have Medicare supplement insurance, and that the premiums are paid regularly. (Have the bills sent to you, if necessary.) Find out how many bank accounts and safe-deposit vaults your parents have.

Have Social Security and pension checks deposited directly into your parents' bank account by means of electronic transfer. Many banks will permit senior citizens to sign a card authorizing it to let another relative know of any unusual account activity. If large checks are drawn against the account, you'll be informed, so you can see if they've been legitimately generated.

Final Thoughts

A durable power of attorney—which covers property—may not be enough. Today, a long-lasting illness may strain your family and drain your assets. You may want to draft a *medical* or *health-care* power of attorney, enabling someone else to make decisions when you no longer can. Similarly, you may want to draw up a living will. Living wills *don't* replace traditional wills, but *do* state the circumstances in which you'd want doctors to withhold or withdraw life-support systems.

Even if you've taken care of all the paperwork—trusts, powers of attorney, living will—you still haven't finished your incompetency planning. You need to explain your plan to your family, especially your spouse and children, or to a long-term companion for whom you wish to provide. Suppose you have three children and you're naming one as a successor trustee. You need to reassure the other two that the one who'll be trustee will have a fiduciary responsibility to watch out for their interests as well.

Planning for incompetency isn't pleasant to think about, but it's an absolute necessity. With luck, after you've taken all the essential steps, you'll live to see triple figures (in more than your checkbook), and still be in full command of your faculties. If so, this will be one plan you'll be *glad* turned out to be a waste of time.

SUMMING UP

• *Revocable* living trusts *don't* provide total asset protection, because it's unlikely you'll transfer all of your assets into a trust.
• Revocable living trusts *should* be supplemented by a power of

attorney that names trusted friends or relatives to handle your finances if necessary.

• *Durable* powers of attorney *will* remain in effect, even if you become incompetent.

• If you *don't* want to have a power of attorney in effect while you're still capable, you may be able to execute a *springing* power that will take effect in certain circumstances.

• Not only should you take steps to guard against *your* incapacity, but also you should make an effort to monitor your *parents'* affairs, to spot signs that they need help with their finances.

• A *medical* power of attorney and a *living* will can make it easier for your family to curtail futile life-support efforts.

Part VII

Courting Disaster

24

An Umbrella Can Let You Smile

Taking Liability Insurance to Excess

Whether or not you have any assets, you're a potential target for financial disaster. If your dog takes a nip at a neighbor's knee, or your teenage son bends a fender in the mall parking lot, you can expect to see a lot of your lawyer in the next few years. Americans love to file lawsuits, plenty of lawyers are willing to work for contingency fees, and juries seem to believe that life begins at seven figures.

In 1993, the *New York Times* published this list of common liability insurance claims paid by Aetna Life and Casualty:

	Percentage of All Claims
Slips and falls	34
Pet bites	19
Other injuries	13
Damage to others' property	13
Violence and altercations	10

Libel and slander	3
Accidental shooting	2
Swimming-pool accidents	1

You need to protect your assets in case any of these events happens on your property, or if a car you own is in an auto accident. Therefore, as mentioned previously, your homeowners and auto insurance both should include *liability coverage.*

Basic coverage for auto insurance is $100,000 worth of liability per person; $300,000 per accident. If you have substantial assets to protect, you might want to increase coverage to $200,000 and $500,000, respectively.

Standard homeowners insurance policies have a $100,000 limit for liability coverage, and that's what most people buy. However, for an extra $15–$25 per year, you can increase coverage to $300,000; for an extra $25–$50, you can increase liability from $100,000 to $500,000. If you have substantial assets, increasing liability insurance to $300,000 or $500,000 is well worth the modest extra cost.

Thanks a Million

Even though the average homeowner's liability claim is around $14,000, State Farm reports, million-dollar judgments have been awarded in cases where someone is severely injured, so $300,000 (or $500,000) worth of auto or homeowners liability coverage may not be enough. If you have $500,000 worth of coverage and lose a $1 million judgment, the extra $500,000 may have to come out of your savings, your pension plan, your house, and other personal assets.

People with assets to lose (or the prospect of sizable future earnings) should protect them with excess-liability insurance, commonly known as *umbrella coverage.* This type of policy kicks in after your *other* liability insurance reaches its limits.

Say that Bob B., a rising young executive, asks his boss over for dinner. His boss's wife becomes acutely ill from the meal, and has to be rushed to the hospital. Not only does she have a long, painful, and costly convalescence, but Bob's boss has to cancel a business trip, and winds up losing a key account. Bob is sued for all this, and the jury finds him at fault to the tune of $1.2 million.

Bob's homeowners policy will provide coverage up to $500,000.

Most fortunately, he is also covered by an umbrella policy—which provides the other $700,000, *plus* his legal costs.

Shelter From the Storm

In addition to increasing your liability coverage, an umbrella policy may expand it. For example, your homeowners policy might *not* cover you for libel or slander claims, but an umbrella policy will. Also, as we've seen in Bob's case, umbrella policies can pay for legal fees if you're sued for an amount in excess of the limits stated in your basic policies. However, some umbrella policies include legal-defense fees as part of their coverage. If you're buying a $1 million umbrella, for instance, look for a policy that covers $1 million worth of excess liability plus legal fees.

Umbrella coverage is surprisingly affordable—mainly because the insurer will be at risk only after your other coverage is used up. In most areas, you can buy $1 million worth of excess-liability insurance for less than $200 per year. If you want to buy instead $2 million worth of coverage, or $3 million, or more, the extra coverage is even less expensive, comparatively speaking, as it increases.

It pays to shop for umbrellas. Some insurers will issue umbrella policies *only* if you buy homeowners and auto insurance from them, *too*. Other companies will give you a better deal if you buy multiple policies (homeowners or auto insurance, or both, plus an umbrella).

Reaching Out

Not only will premiums vary from insurer to insurer, but coverage may be different, too. Some umbrella policies, for example, have very low limits for uninsured-motorist coverage (a $25,000 ceiling, for example).

Besides libel- and slander protection, an umbrella policy should cover claims of mental anguish, defamation of character, and invasion of privacy. They should cover you for liability associated with your residences, autos, watercraft, and recreational vehicles. If you travel abroad, be sure your umbrella gives you international protection—some policies are limited to the United States and Canada. If a policy *doesn't* have coverage you specifically want, ask for an amendment that will either add it or override the exclusion.

Unfortunately, umbrellas won't keep all the raindrops from falling on your head. They cover *personal*, rather than business or professional, liability. Thus, you may need even *more* liability coverage than you suspect you do, depending on how you earn your living.

SUMMING UP

• In recent years, million-dollar-plus judgments have become common in United States courts—especially in personal-injury cases.

• People with substantial assets are frequent targets of personal-injury suits.

• Ordinarily, homeowners' and auto insurance provide liability coverage, but seldom more than $300,000 or $500,000 worth.

• You can buy excess-liability insurance in order to provide coverage for larger amounts.

• Umbrella insurance, as it's known, generally starts at $1 million worth of coverage.

• The cost of excess-liability insurance probably will be only a few hundred dollars per year.

• Shop carefully for umbrella policies, paying special attention to what's covered and what's excluded.

• Even if you buy umbrella insurance, you *also* may need to carry business or professional (such as malpractice) liability insurance.

25

Sharing the Wealth

Joint Ownership Can Be a Wrenching Experience

If you're married, you probably own your home jointly. Officially, title is held in *joint tenancy* or *joint ownership with right of survivorship*. This may be comforting for you and your spouse—but in fact it might not be the best choice.

Technically, if you and your spouse or significant other are joint owners, you each own 100 percent of the property. When one dies, there is only one 100 percent owner left. And that's it. Nothing you state in either a will or a trust can override joint ownership.

Joint ownership has its virtues. At the death of the first spouse, transfer is fast and cheap: No probate, no lawyers, little paperwork. No taxes will be owed. If you have a simple family situation with a small estate, obviously joint ownership can make sense.

But (alas!) life isn't always simple. Suppose, for example, that you are divorced and remarried. You live with your second (or other suc-ceeding) spouse in a house valued at $200,000. (In some parts of

California and the Northeast, you may very well live in a $400,000 house.)

If you die first, a jointly owned house goes entirely to your spouse—all $200,000 or $300,000 or $400,000 worth, or whatever. Any children you have, by any previous marriage, won't get any of that house—which may well have been your largest asset. Your spouse, then, is free to leave that house to his or her children, or indeed anyone else he or she chooses.

Suppose you own a vacation house, or investment real estate. If that's jointly owned, the same problems can arise. In fact, *anything* that's jointly owned, such as mutual-fund shares or a brokerage account, can lead to this trap.

Or, suppose you jointly own assets with someone who is not a relative, by blood or marriage. If you die first, those assets will automatically pass to your co-owner. If you want to make some other disposition, you're out of luck.

Out of Control

As you can see, joint ownership means both a loss of control and a lack of flexibility. This is a particular handicap if your estate is large enough to make estate taxes a concern.

Let's say, for example, that you and your spouse (a first marriage with children) have a total of $1.2 million in assets. You divide the assets equally, through spousal gifts, so that each spouse owns $500,000 worth, plus a $200,000 house in joint ownership. At the death of whichever spouse dies first, $500,000 is to pass to your children. Because of the $600,000 federal estate-tax exemption, *no* estate tax would be due.

The surviving spouse, though, now has $500,000 plus a $200,000 house. If he or she dies the next day, with a $700,000 estate, the children will owe $37,000 to the IRS. That's $37,000 that, with better planning, could have been in their pockets.

The larger the estate you have, and the more property held jointly, the greater the tax problems you're likely to run into. Those problems will be even more difficult to solve if you *also* have a sizable retirement plan with your spouse named as beneficiary—which usually *is* the case.

Tax Tactics

Besides estate-tax problems, joint ownership can cause income-tax problems. Take our example of the $1.2 million couple with the $200,000 house. Suppose the couple's "basis" (cost, for tax purposes) in the house is $50,000. After the death of the first spouse, the survivor sells the house for $200,000—the market price—because he or she intends to move to a small apartment.

Under current tax law, the half belonging to the spouse who died first is "stepped up" to $100,000, but the survivor still has a $25,000 basis for his or her half. Thus, he or she has a $75,000 taxable gain. (It's true that there's a $125,000 exclusion from these gains for homeowners over age fifty-five. But that won't help if either is under fifty-five, or if the jointly owned property is something other than a primary residence.)

By comparison, if the house had been owned entirely by the spouse who died first, and it was left to his or her survivor, the entire house would get a step-up. The widower could sell the house for $200,000 and owe *no* income tax on *any* capital gain.

Double Exposure

Another drawback to joint ownership is exposure to creditors. If *either* co-owner owes money, the *entire* property might be seized, even though the other co-owner doesn't! This drawback applies to any property owned jointly; if joint ownership is between *nonspouses*, the problems may be even *greater*.

Suppose you and your partner jointly own the building in which your garment business is located. If you die first, the building automatically passes to him or her. Your family is frozen out. Worse, half the value of the building is included in *your* taxable estate. Your family could wind up with a huge estate-tax bill for property that's going to your business partner!

Moreover, joint ownership between nonspouses may create a *gift-tax* obligation. (That won't be a problem for spouses, who can make unlimited gifts to each other, tax-free.) Suppose your spouse dies, so you sell the old family residence and buy a retirement home in Florida. Title is held jointly between you and your daughter. Assuming you paid the full $100,000 for the new house, you may have made a

$50,000 gift to your daughter—which would trigger a gift tax. Again, at your death, the house will automatically pass to your daughter, which may mean a smaller inheritance for your son. Plus, your daughter will get only a half step-up in basis (see above), which could lead to income taxes if she sells the house after your death.

Keep It Simple

If joint ownership is so fraught with perils, what can you do about that? First, you can always discuss title to a major asset (real estate, securities) with a local attorney. Different states have different rules—especially when it comes to taxes.

However, you may want to own property in *fee simple* (completely owned by one person) or in *tenancy in common*. In most states, the latter works just like joint ownership, except that each co-owner has the right to leave his or her share of the property to whomever he or she wishes. With either fee-simple or tenancy-in-common ownership, you generally have more control, more flexibility, and a greater opportunity to transfer your wealth in the way you prefer.

SUMMING UP

• Married couples often hold property jointly; joint ownership may be used by nonspouses as well.
• Joint ownership is simple, facilitating transfer of property after the death of one owner.
• Jointly owned property must however pass to the surviving owner, a move which can rob the deceased's estate and heirs of more than flexibility.
• Joint ownership may hamper tax planning, too.
• Unless your family situation is very straightforward, your property should be held in *fee simple* or in *tenancy in common* forms which give you more flexibility and more control.

26

Filing for the Future

Coping When Personal Bankruptcy Is Inevitable

What happens when your income plummets, yet you're stuck with debts from a happier time? When your liabilities exceed your assets, you're *insolvent*. You can try to negotiate with your creditors and consult with a "credit counselor." However, when all else fails, you may be forced to file for *personal bankruptcy*. In the United States, such filings are estimated at around one million per year.

Even though it's increasingly common, *don't* take a personal bankruptcy filing lightly. There are severe financial and psychological consequences. Bankruptcy is your last resort, not your first. But if you *are* forced into bankruptcy, go in with your eyes open. You may be able to retain substantial assets, and the damage to your credit rating may not be as severe as you'd expect.

The federal bankruptcy code contains several "Chapters" under which you can file. Many borrowers prefer Chapter 13, which can be filed as often as necessary. In Chapter 13, you're protected from creditors' demands while a court works out a repayment schedule—typically three to five years.

However, Chapter 13 is limited to debtors with less than $100,000 in *unsecured* debt and up to $350,000 in *secured* debt. (If your debts are larger, you can file under the more complicated Chapter 11, which usually is used by troubled businesses.)

The most common alternative to Chapter 13 is Chapter 7, which can be utilized no more than once every six years. When Chapter 7 is filed, all cosigners *must* make good on their promises to repay loans. Assuming there still are debts outstanding, you have to sell your assets and pay off the remaining creditors—who typically receive partial payments. If a Chapter 13 payment schedule isn't met, one's bankruptcy likely will be converted to Chapter 7.

If permitted by the six-year rule, you might consider (supposing that you're involved) a Chapter 20 filing—7 *plus* 13. First, you file under Chapter 7, and wipe out *most* of your obligations. Some debts (e.g., student loans, child support, alimony, certain taxes) *can't* be discharged in bankruptcy, however—so you can then file a Chapter 13, to stretch out the payments.

Holding On

Fortunately, even a Chapter 7 filing won't strip you completely: Even bankrupts are permitted to keep *some* assets. In fact, depending on your state, you may be able to keep a personal residence, life-insurance policies, annuities, IRAs, and other retirement plans, out of the reach of your creditors.

Some states are much more generous than others. Florida and Texas, for example, are known to be "debtor friendly." In some well-publicized cases, people have moved to these states and purchased large houses or annuities before filing for bankruptcy.

A New York court decision may afford yet *more* protection for bankrupts. Two restaurant owners filed for bankruptcy, owing $120,000 on bank loans they had personally guaranteed. Their main assets were their homes, jointly owned with spouses.

The usual practice in New York had been to sell the bankrupts' half-interests to their spouses at below-market prices. The proceeds could then be applied to the debt repayment. Instead, the bank asked the *bankruptcy trustee* to sell the houses on the open market, and deliver half the proceeds to the bank. However, a federal bankruptcy judge ruled that such a forced sale is unconstitutional, *even though* it's in the bankruptcy law, because it would jeopardize the spouses' property rights.

This decision, if followed by other courts, could provide nationwide protection to couples with jointly held property. As one lawyer has said, "There's no longer a reason to move to Florida in a bankruptcy situation."

In bankruptcy planning, remember the line between *transferring* and *shifting* assets. The former usually means giving your assets to a relative so they'll be protected from creditors. Such transfers, within a year or so of a bankruptcy filing, may well be disregarded by a bankruptcy court.

Shifting assets, on the other hand, means repositioning assets so they'll be safe within your *own* possession. Depending on your state, you might want to buy an annuity, or pay off a home mortgage, with cash in the bank. A certain amount of shifting is permitted—but pigs get slaughtered, as the saying goes.

Separation Pay

Even those who haven't been profligate may find themselves in a bankruptcy situation. Becky S. of Austin, Texas, for example, divorced her husband and wound up with a nasty postnuptial gift: her husband's $1 million tax obligation, payable to the IRS. Becky, who signed the joint tax returns, was on the hook. She offered to pay the IRS $100,000 over five years, but the IRS didn't accept. The only answer was a bankruptcy filing.

The first step to take if you're considering bankruptcy is to ask friends and associates for the name of a local lawyer who specializes in bankruptcy filings. Such a lawyer likely will help you shelter as much as possible *without* incurring the wrath of the bankruptcy court.

Is bankruptcy the end of the world? Not really. Officially, a bankruptcy filing stays on your credit rating for ten years. However, some lenders are willing to work with bankrupts after a year or two. One Purdue University study found that 16 percent of bankrupts get credit in *one* year, and 53 percent within *five* years. The best sources are consumer finance companies, retail stores, and auto dealers. You also might be able to obtain a *secured credit card*, backing up your credit line with a deposit in the issuer's bank.

One common ploy is to keep one credit card current, or to bring it current before the filing. That issuer, then, isn't listed as a creditor, and may not find out about the bankruptcy—so the card can still be used. (The legality of this maneuver is in doubt, to say the least, so we don't recommend it.)

Don't neglect the *personal* side of a bankruptcy filing. All of your family members will simply have to learn to do without even little luxuries—at least for a while. There also can be guilt feelings, blame-spreading, and loss of friendships. If you talk with everyone and explain the situation, however, conflicts usually can be brought out into the open and dealt with. In fact, some areas even have "insolvency support groups," to help with coping. A lawyer specializing in bankruptcy filings should be able to tell you if there's one nearby, and how to contact it.

SUMMING UP

• When your debts exceed your assets, you're *insolvent,* and you may find protection by filing for *bankruptcy.*
• Bankruptcy filings should be a last resort, because they cannot help but have severe repercussions.
• *Chapter 13* of the bankruptcy code is limited to small debtors, who are protected from creditors while they work out a repayment schedule—usually up to five years.
• In a *Chapter 7* filing, you have to sell off assets and repay creditors. They typically receive partial payments.
• Depending on the state of their residency, bankrupts are permitted to keep *some* assets (and rather valuable ones, at that), such as homes, retirement plans, and insurance policies.
• Shifting assets from an unprotected to a protected category before filing for bankruptcy may be acceptable, but transferring assets to friends or family members generally won't protect them.
• Although a bankruptcy stays on your credit rating for ten years, you may be able to get credit sooner—perhaps from a retailer or consumer finance company.

27

Family Value

Shelter Assets, Keep Control With a Family Limited Partnership

You don't have to be an avid newspaper reader to come across stories of outrageous court decisions in the United States in the late twentieth century. Reportedly, a ninety-one-year-old woman was found liable for $950,000 because she loaned money to her grandnephew, who bought a car with that money, wrecked it, and injured a passenger. Also, a man who tried to collect a $50,000 loan to a fellow church member was hit by a $2.7 million jury award. And a retailer lost a $1 million suit to a man who claimed he suffered a heart attack while pulling the starter cord on a lawn mower he bought at the other fellow's store. And so on.

If you have assets that mean anything at all, you're a target. Liability insurance, (described in Chapter 24 of this book) is a *must*, but it still won't cover everything. If you have substantial assets, you may need to take extraordinary measures to protect them. Moreover, people with the latter kind of assets face substantial estate-tax liability (which we'll cover in Part IX). *Family limited partnerships*, increasingly popular these days, can enable you to reduce your taxable estate as well as your exposure to creditors, yet retain control of your assets.

All in the Family

A *limited partnership* consists of two classes of partners: *general* (GP) and *limited* (LP). The general partner makes all management decisions and bears liability for partnership debt. The limited partners, who cannot participate in management, enjoy the same limited liability as corporate stockholders.

Suppose you form the Williams Family Limited Partnership, consisting of a one percent GP interest and a 99 percent LP interest. A newly formed corporation that you control (or that's controlled by you and your spouse) might be the general partner, while the limited-partnership interests also are held by you (and possibly your spouse). As long as the corporation acting as general partner has some capital and is more than a shell, it likely will shield you from liabilities incurred by the partnership.

Next, you retitle assets so that the Williams Family Limited Partnership owns your stocks and mutual funds, investment real-estate, and other assets. There generally are no tax consequences for this ownership transfer. Essentially, you're shifting assets from one pocket to another.

A *family* limited partnership can hold just about anything except retirement plans and shares of S corporations. However, if you transfer your family home into a limited partnership, you won't be able to deduct mortgage interest on your personal tax return.

Depending on your situation, you might want more than one family limited partnership. H&H Bagels of New York, for example, is owned by the First Toro Family Limited Partnership. Founder Helmer Toro created other limited partnerships in order to own his bakery and the H&H trademark. Thus, if one of his assets is threatened, the others will be insulated.

After the family limited partnership is in place, you can transfer limited-partnership interests or partial interests. In most cases, the transfers will be to your children or grandchildren.

With no gift-tax consequences, you can shift up to $10,000 worth of assets per year, per recipient, to any number of recipients. For a married couple, the limit is $20,000. In addition, you can give up to

$600,000, or $1.2 million worth of assets in larger chunks—this strategy *would not* trigger a gift tax but *would* reduce or eliminate your estate-tax exemption.

Less Equals More

Thanks to a 1993 IRS ruling on minority discounts, you may make even larger gifts—without owing tax—because the limited-partnership interests given away have *no control* over the assets. Suppose your family limited partnership contains a family corporation valued at $2 million, with 200,000 shares outstanding. Normally, each share would be worth $10, so a married couple could give away 2,000 shares per year ($20,000 worth), gift-tax-free.

However, if you transfer limited-partnership interests with no control over the business, a third-party appraisal might state that each of the transferred shares is worth *less* than $10. Thus, you can give away *more* shares. In many cases, the IRS will concede a 15 percent minority discount. If you have supporting evidence, such as an outside appraisal, you may even be able to sustain a 35 percent or 45 percent discount.

Say you have solid grounds for a 33.3 percent minority discount. Instead of giving away 2,000 shares per recipient per year, as in our example, you could give away 3,000 shares and still stay within the $20,000 gift-tax limit.

Number of shares	3,000
Nominal value per share	$10
Total	$30,000
Minority discount (33.3%)	($10,000)
Net value of gift	$20,000

By the same reasoning, you might transfer $1.8 million worth of shares (90 percent of your $2 million company), use a 33.3 percent discount to knock down the value to $1.2 million, and owe *no* gift tax.

Over time, you might transfer the entire 99 percent limited-partnership interest to your children and grandchildren, *free* of gift tax. And those assets *won't* be included in your taxable estate. Also, even though you give away as much as 99 percent of those assets, you're still in control of the general-partnership interest! You continue to manage the business, the real estate, the securities portfolio, and the like. In fact, you can pay *yourself* a salary for running your family limited partnership.

In addition, when you transfer interests to other family members, you may be able to retain *qualified preferred payments* (income that comes before anyone else gets paid) from partnership income. This will give you additional income which won't increase the tax on your Social Security benefits in retirement, while the value of the qualified preferred payments will reduce the taxable value of the transferred interests.

After your salary and any qualified preferred payments are accounted for, the remaining partnership income flows through to the partners. Your partnership agreement might even state that 99 percent of the income goes to the 99 percent limited-partnership interest. If your children and grandchildren own the limited-partnership interests, *they'll* owe the tax—hopefully in a lower bracket than yours. Yet, though you avoid both the income and estate taxes, you still have control over those assets!

Behind the Barricades

Moreover, your personal wealth is less vulnerable inside a family limited partnership. Or, you might want to set up a family limited partnership before you get married, as an alternative to a prenuptial agreement. You can thereby protect your assets against possible future divorce proceedings.

Suppose a carpenter hurts himself while working on your house, and sues you. He might win a huge judgment against you or your spouse that includes the rights to a share of the partnership. However, if your assets are in a properly structured family limited partnership, he generally won't be able to *seize* them, but rather will have to wait until assets or income are distributed. And, he can't either sell the asset he's been awarded, or borrow against it. Instead, the successful plaintiff likely will obtain a *charging order*.

You, in control of the general partner, can decide not to make distributions to the limited partners, even while you continue to receive a salary. Under the tax code, the limited partners (including your creditor) will have to pay taxes on any taxable income that the partnership generates, even though no cash is distributed. The thought of having to pay tax on phantom income, year after year, can be a powerful tool to force a creditor to settle for less—often pennies on the dollar.

If you already have a trust established, for estate-planning reasons, partnership interests *can* go into that trust, providing yet *another* layer of asset protection.

An Ounce of Prevention

What's the down side? Family limited partnerships are *expensive*. Expect to pay a lawyer around $3,000 up front, for legal drafting fees, plus up to $1,000 per year for ongoing administration, including tax preparation. If your affairs are more complicated, the legal costs may be even higher. Often, though, you can offset some of these costs by cutting back on your liability insurance.

Also, don't forget that the general partner bears partnership *liabilities*. If the assets you transfer into a family limited partnership are not likely to generate liability, you can be an individual general partner, or you and your spouse can be co-general partners. However, if there's either real estate or an operating business in the partnership, you *should* have a corporate general partner, for additional protection.

Another problem is the legal doctrine of *fraudulent conveyance*. To hold up, an asset transfer can't have the purpose of hindering, delaying, or defrauding creditors. You must be financially solvent both before and after the transaction.

If someone has a *claim* against you, it may not help to set up a family limited partnership: A judge most likely will say that you still own the assets. Similarly, establishing a family limited partnership to protect assets against an impending claim may not work. If an action is filed a few months after a partnership is created, the transaction probably won't pass the "smell test."

You need to strike *before* the iron gets hot. If you set up a family limited partnership now, you're not likely to be charged with fraud if a creditor comes after you several years from now. (One court decision has held that it is okay to transfer assets from the reach of *possible* creditors, but not from *probable* creditors.)

Document your reasons for setting up a family limited partnership. Estate-tax reduction will be accepted; creditor avoidance might not be. So get an opinion letter from your tax pro, saying you're setting up your family limited partnership as part of an estate plan.

A family limited partnership is *not* an absolute barrier against claims. For example, in one pertinent case, a creditor was allowed to attach and sell a limited partner's interest in order to satisfy an old judgment. Nor is a family limited partnership a license to steal with impunity, dodging legitimate creditors.

However, if your *personal* wealth is threatened, a family limited partnership *can* enhance your bargaining position. With most of your assets inside a limited partnership, beyond the easy reach of creditors, you'll be a smaller target. A claimant—and the claimant's lawyer— may be more willing to settle on reasonable, but *not* outrageous, terms.

SUMMING UP

• Family limited partnerships enable you to remove assets from your personal possession while retaining control.
• You can transfer assets to a limited partnership, then transfer the limited-partnership interests to family members—probably best your children and grandchildren.
• As long as you control the general-partnership interest, you control *all* the assets in the partnership.
• The assets you transfer to family members will be out of your taxable estate.
• Assets held inside a limited partnership will have substantial creditor protection, which may discourage claimants or lead to favorable settlements.
• You'll have to pay sizable legal fees to set up and maintain a family limited partnership, but it can allow you to enjoy advantages even beyond those discussed herein.
• If you're interested in setting up a limited partnership, you should act before you've been sued or face a likely suit.

28

Trusts, Un-Bustable

Protect Your Assets, Cut Taxes
With Irrevocable Trusts

How do you keep your assets from being consumed by divorce actions, lawsuits, business failures, catastrophic medical bills, or any of the many other means our society provides for others to put their hands into your pocket? Certain asset-protection steps are basic, such as buying liability insurance. Too, if you operate a business, you should use a corporate form to limit your liability. And family limited partnerships can help you reduce estate-tax liability while shielding your wealth.

Moreover, if you're really serious about asset protection, you should consider shifting assets into a trust. Property held in a properly drafted trust will belong to the trust, *not* to you—so it won't be vulnerable to assaults on your *personal* assets.

Revocable living trusts (covered in Chapter 22) are fine for transferring assets in case of your incompetency or after your death, without the time and expense of probate. However, such trusts generally *won't* work for asset protection. Since at any time you can revoke this type of trust and reclaim the assets, they are still considered *yours*.

For more asset protection, you'll need an *irrevocable trust*. As the name suggests, these trusts are for keeps. Once they're set up and funded, *you lose control* of the trust's assets—and you can't revoke the trust, or change its terms. Because the assets are beyond your control, they're generally beyond the reach of creditors, too—at times a most helpful limitation.

But isn't this cutting off your nose to spite your face? Your creditors can't get at your money, but you can't, *either*. Ah, but that's not necessarily the case! Working with an experienced attorney, you may be able to structure a trust that will protect your assets *even* as you continue to benefit. And you probably can set up a trust that will provide for your family—if not directly for yourself.

Hands Off

One possibility is a *charitable remainder trust*. You can get a lifetime income from this trust; appreciated assets you donate can be sold *without* generating a tax on the capital gains. Plus, assets in a bona fide charitable trust likely will be safe from creditors. However: After the death of the "income beneficiaries," *all* the assets will go to charity, rather than to your family.

A more common situation arises when you want to protect your own assets now and provide for your family later. (In some states, retirement funds, cash-value life insurance, or annuities are protected from creditors, so you might want to keep enough money in these vehicles for your own income, and transfer the rest to an irrevocable trust for safety.) You might establish a trust naming your spouse, or a grown child, or a trusted financial adviser as a trustee. Given such, although *you* won't have direct access to your money, friends or relatives can get their hands on it if necessary.

One asset-protection technique is the use of a *lifetime QTIP trust*. In such a trust, your *spouse* is entitled to all the income for life, while *you* can name the ultimate beneficiaries—usually your children. Naturally, the money that comes to your spouse can be used to buy groceries, make mortgage payments, etc.—so this may work well if you have a *strong* marriage.

Another approach is to set up a *spendthrift trust* whereby the trustee has a great deal of leeway in handling funds, and the beneficiaries can't transfer their interests, borrow against them, and the like. In general, the more discretionary the trustee's power, the more creditor-proof the trust will be.

Sprinkle With Care

Family circumstances can complicate any asset-protection plan. Let's say you want to protect your assets, but you're not sure whether you— and your spouse—will have enough to live on if you put most of your property into a trust. You're reluctant to part with assets you might need later.

Even if you decide to give away some assets, to whom would you give them? To the child who already has a family and a promising career, the child who is likely to have lifelong problems, or the child who is still too young to assess? And, once you give away assets, how can you be sure they'll be well conserved?

With a *sprinkle trust*, you can provide for each family member according to his or her needs, while you avoid gift- and estate taxes. You can name a number of trust beneficiaries, including your spouse, your children, and your grandchildren. The trust documents likely will state that the income from the trust assets, and possibly the trust assets themselves, can be used for the support and maintenance of the beneficiaries. *No* beneficiary is entitled to trust income as a matter of right. Instead, distribution of trust income and principal is *entirely* at the discretion of the trustee.

The key to a sprinkle trust, then, is the selection of a good trustee or trustees. You or your spouse *can't* be trustees, and neither can a child or grandchild. You may choose an *in-law*, a *friend*, a *professional adviser*, or an *institutional trustee*. Besides your absolute faith in the trustee's integrity, his or her common sense and knowledge of your family situation are the paramount qualifications.

If you choose cotrustees, try to pick people who are compatible, so that deadlocks can be avoided. Include a provision for selecting a successor trustee in case an original trustee dies or resigns.

Once assets are transferred to the trust, the trustee runs the show. He or she has a broad latitude in distributing trust assets to the beneficiaries. The trustee might, for example, distribute money to your son, say to help with a down payment on a house, or to finance his daughter's private schooling. If your daughter needs special medical care, the trustee can provide the necessary money. If your own fortunes suffer a reversal and you run short of retirement income, the trustee can distribute funds to your spouse.

Thus, if you have the right trustee, a sprinkle trust can give you the best of all such worlds. You protect your assets, you avoid gift- and estate taxes, you provide for your family's future needs, and you have a prudent trustee (*required* to act responsibly) rather than your family members handling the assets.

Tax Bracket Arbitrage

There may also be income-tax advantages to a sprinkle trust. Say you have a $600,000 securities portfolio, throwing off $30,000 a year in taxable income. In your possession, that $30,000 is added to all of your other income, and taxed at 40 percent or more, including state and local taxes. Your trustee, though, may be distributing the funds to lower-bracket recipients. Posit that your daughter, a banker, has a son in college. Money needed for education might be distributed to your grandson, who is in a lower tax bracket than your daughter and son-in-law.

Moreover, the trust itself has a tax bracket, which means that a surplus (income minus distributions) may be taxed at only 15 percent or 28 percent. In 1994, for example, trust income up to $1,500 qualified for a 15 percent rate, a threshold that will increase annually to keep up with inflation.

A sprinkle trust can solve a host of asset-protection, tax, and family problems. However, consider a sprinkle trust *only* if you're certain that your trustee will serve well, *and* if an experienced attorney handles the trust creation.

Little Words Mean a Lot

When you establish an irrevocable trust, one wrong word can ruin all your asset-protection time and expense. Suppose you create a trust that will provide lifetime income for your spouse, after your death. You want to keep the trust assets out of your spouse's estate, as well as out of yours. At his or her death, the assets either will pass to your children, or will stay in trust for the benefit of your children and grandchildren.

Your spouse is worried that the trust income won't be enough for him or her to live comfortably. Your spouse wants to be able to use the principal, if more money is needed. Therefore, some provision is made for him or her to have access to the trust assets. There's a trap here: If the survivor's access to trust principal is too broad, the assets will be considered under that person's control, and included in his or her taxable estate.

The Tax Court's 1991 decision in the Estate of Norman Vissering case illustrates what can happen. Vissering's mother set up a trust to pay lifetime income to herself. After her death, the trust was to pay lifetime income to her son, Norman Vissering. Other family members were also named as beneficiaries, eligible to receive trust distributions. Norman Vissering was cotrustee, along with a bank.

Many years after his mother's death, Norman Vissering developed Alzheimer's disease and was declared incapacitated. He died a few months later. The IRS asserted that the trust assets were part of his taxable estate.

The case went to Tax Court, where the IRS pointed to the trust provision giving the trustee the authority to use the principal for the "continued comfort, support, maintenance, or education" of the beneficiaries. This provision, it contended, gave cotrustee Vissering a "general power of appointment," meaning control over the assets. If this *general* power of appointment existed, the trust assets would be includible in his taxable estate.

Vissering's estate argued that the power of appointment was limited, *not* general. The tax code specifically states that the power to invade the trust for a beneficiary's "health, education, support, or maintenance" is a *limited* power, and thus does *not* result in inclusion.

An Un-Comfortable Decision

However, Vissering's estate lost solely because the word *comfort* was included in the trust. "Comfort" goes beyond "health, education, support, or maintenance." Because of the trust wording in this case, cotrustee Vissering could distribute the trust assets however he wanted for the comfort of beneficiaries. Therefore, said the Tax Court, the assets were under his control, and as such were includible in his taxable estate.

The IRS has specifically stated that the three words comfort, welfare, and happiness result in broader powers, and may result in inclusion. On the other hand, the IRS has *blessed* four *other* words—health, education, support, and maintenance—in the case of situations where the trust may need to be invaded. Those words are the legal equivalent of safe harbors. Any other words are invitations to disaster on the rocky shoals. In this case, that one no-no word—comfort—resulted in inclusion and cost the estate over $700,000 in estate taxes that needn't have been paid otherwise.

Moreover, the IRS has added the word *care* to the terms conveying broader powers than permitted. (Such words as *catastrophe* and *emergency* also should be avoided.) In truth, none of these words adds very much to the powers implied by the acceptable health-education-support-maintenance vocabulary list.

Vissering was officially incapacitated and could make no distributions at the time of his death. The court included the assets anyway, because Vissering had not been removed as trustee, and still technically retained the trustee's powers. Similarly, the fact that Vissering was cotrustee with a bank did not sway the court. The bank was not an "adverse" party having an interest in the trust assets opposed to Vissering's.

Whenever a trust beneficiary is also a trustee, the danger of inclusion is present. It may actually *help* to name a cotrustee with an adverse interest—such as another trust beneficiary. Even if a trust beneficiary is *not* a trustee, assets may be includible *if* the beneficiary can dismiss the trustee and name a replacement. That is, the beneficiary has control over the assets *because* he or she can appoint a friendly trustee.

Often, the beneficiaries' ability to remove trustees may be their sole leverage in assuring that they receive quality service. Therefore, if your estate planning calls for giving trust beneficiaries this leverage, you need to be sure that the power of appointment is limited rather than broad. Check the wording in existing trust documents and in your will, if it calls for a *testamentary trust* (a trust that goes into effect after death) to be created.

The Sooner, the Better

Creating an irrevocable trust won't protect your assets if they're *already* in jeopardy. If a worker falls off your roof today and you establish a trust tomorrow, the courts likely won't grant the trust assets any protection. But if you set up a trust *now* and run into a difficult situation in five years, the assets may well be out of creditors' reach. In any event, you should be able to show another reason for establishing the trust, besides asset protection—estate tax reduction, for example, or care for a family member.

Once you've made the decision to establish a trust, funding it can be a problem, however. Except for charitable trusts, gifts to irrevocable trusts are subject to gift-tax limitations. You can give away $10,000 per year per recipient ($20,000 from a married couple), but that won't do much if you want to protect *substantial* assets. Besides, you have to jump through a few hoops in order for gifts to trusts to qualify for the gift-tax exclusion.

Instead, you might want to use your *unified credit*. As of this writing, you can give away up to $600,000 worth of assets to such a trust, free of gift tax. If your spouse goes along with the gift, you can shift up to $1.2 million, tax-free. Making large gifts now *will* cut into (or use up) your $600,000 exemption from estate taxes, but doing so while it's still valid might just be a good idea: A revenue-starved Congress could trim this exemption at any time!

Once assets are shifted to an irrevocable trust, they're out of your taxable estate. If you transfer assets that may appreciate (stocks, real estate), any future growth *also* is out of your estate. Of course, "irrevocable" means that you can't change your mind: Once you make the transfer, the assets no longer belong to *you*.

Because such trust assets no longer belong to you, they should be protected—and probably can be, provided you work with a knowledgeable lawyer. At the very least, you'll be erecting a substantial barrier between your assets and the scavengers. When the contingency-fee lawyers come sniffing around, looking for easy prey, they may decide to pick on someone else if you have your assets snugly tucked away in an irrevocable trust.

SUMMING UP

• When you transfer assets into an irrevocable trust, they're out of your control, so they're also likely out of the reach of creditors.
• Transfers to irrevocable trusts also move assets out of your taxable estate.
• Such trusts can be structured so that your family members have access, even if *you* don't.
• Often, you'll need to rely on a trustee who'll make distributions where the money is needed.
• When you set up an irrevocable trust, take care that the trustee

can provide for the beneficiaries' "health," "education," "support," and "maintenance," but *not* for their "comfort," "happiness," "welfare," or "care."

• The sooner you set up an irrevocable trust, before there are real threats to your assets, the greater your protection will be.

29

Out of the Country, Out of Reach

Offshore Trusts May Provide the Ultimate in Asset Protection

For Dr. X, the trouble began with a story in the *Wall Street Journal*, announcing his plans to open a chain of bargain-priced clinics. After that article appeared, his not-so-professional colleagues put out a contract on him, Dr. X asserts. There was a lengthy exposé on a local TV station in the city where he practices, followed by a closetful of lawsuits. "I probably spent more time giving depositions than anyone else in America," he later recalled.

Whatever the cause, the doctor definitely faced a daunting calendar of days in court. Not only were more than 150 suits filed against him, but fifteen were uninsured. By his lights, they were nuisance suits. Still, the lawyers he first consulted took these claims seriously, telling him that he might wind up paying hundreds of thousands of dollars.

After years of fruitless expense and aggravation, Dr. X changed lawyers: He hired a law firm that specializes in shifting assets to idyllic isles, out of the reach of rapacious creditors. This firm helped Dr. X set up a trust in the Cook Islands, south of Hawaii. Into the trust went those assets which reasonable people might want: bank accounts, stocks, bonds. Remaining in Dr. X's name were mainly real-estate limited-partnership interests of uncertain value. If everything were to go well, they might pay off nicely for his children and grandchildren.

Once his liquid assets were in the South Pacific, Dr. X turned to the various plaintiffs. He told them to take their pick of the assets he had left. Or, they could take $1,000 in cash. Most of the claimants took the cash—he asserted that he settled all fifteen uninsured cases for under $20,000.

Strip Poker

You don't have to be an imperiled physician to love offshore trusts. One semiretired business owner, for example, had invested in a strip shopping center that defaulted on a $3.5 million mortgage. As a partner, this investor probably could have been held liable for the entire amount. But he set up a Cook Islands trust and transferred assets there—and eventually the lender settled for $150,000.

Today, it's not hard to think of ways in which you can be wiped out. If you're a professional or a business owner (or even a spouse in a shaky marriage), your personal assets may be vulnerable to large judgments. Traditional means of protection—liability insurance, incorporation—*aren't* fail-safe. The courts are continually recognizing new "rights" for plaintiffs, at the expense of people trying to hold on to their wealth.

For these reasons and more, affluent Americans are turning to a variety of preservation strategies, of which the offshore asset-protection trust (APT) may be the most formidable. In essence, by using this strategy, your assets are held in a trust set up *outside* the reach of the U.S. judicial system. A creditor must prevail in a *foreign* court before being able to lay his hands on those assets. In some overseas jurisdictions, you can retain control *and* enjoy the benefits of trust assets—even while they're protected.

One law firm that has become a leader in the field discovered the virtues of APTs when its own malpractice-insurance premiums skyrocketed. In 1984, despite a clean history, the firm's insurer raised the premium from \$10,000 to \$150,000 while reducing coverage from \$10 million to \$1 million. In response, the principals shifted personal assets to a trust on the Isle of Man, a British Commonwealth member in the Irish Sea. Many Americans like to deal with Manx trusts because they're comfortable with the location, the language, and the political and economic stability.

After the law firm (Engel & Rudman, based in Denver) began creating Manx trusts for wealthy clients, Cook Islands officials asked the firm to help create a state-of-the-art law on asset protection there, in the late 1980s. Since then, many jurisdictions have acquired enhanced-asset protection, including the Bahamas, Belize, the British Virgins, the Caymans, Cyprus, Gibraltar, Jersey, the Turks, and the Caicos—all from the onetime Tax Haven Hall of Fame and all now determined to become asset-protection havens. Nevertheless, the greatest protection may be available in the Cook Islands.

The Cook Islands International Trust Act prohibits the enforcement of foreign judgments, so litigants are forced to commence actions *de novo* ("from scratch") in a Cook Islands court. In the Cook Islands, therefore, judgments issued by U.S. courts *aren't* automatically recognized, as they are in most of the world. Instead, a claimant must hire an attorney who practices in the Cook Islands, and that attorney must be paid, win or lose—no contingency fees are permitted there. In court, the burden of proof rests on the creditor, who must satisfy a criminal standard (beyond a reasonable doubt) in order to prevail.

The Cook Islands law also addresses the aforementioned issue of *fraudulent conveyance*. If you transfer assets merely to put them out of the reach of creditors, the transaction will be considered fraud, and disregarded. The same outcome generally results if you transfer assets merely to thwart potential creditors—the visitor who's sure to sue you next week for the broken hip suffered while tripping on your dog's bone and falling down your steps.

Fraudulent conveyance is less likely to be a problem if you use an APT as a vaccine rather than as a cure. Establish a trust, and shift assets while you have no major claims outstanding, or likely claims pending. If you shift assets in 1995 and your visitor stumbles in 1999, it will be hard to make the case that assets were transferred to thwart future bone-trippers. Moreover, the Cook Islands has a statute of limitations on fraudulent conveyance: One year after the transfer of assets, or two years after the underlying cause of action (such as negligence), fraudulent conveyance can't be charged. By the time a plaintiff finds out where the money is and files an action, the statute of limitations may prevent the suit.

However, most people procrastinate, so transfers are made *after* creditors' actions are likely, or even are under way already. In these situations, it's more difficult to avoid a fraudulent-conveyance claim. You'll probably be better off if you stay solvent—at least on paper—while moving the most tempting assets out of easy reach.

Pull Up the Drawbridge

Establishing an APT won't allow you to cheat or maim your fellows with impunity. Instead, the idea is to reduce the financial profile you present to would-be claimants. A lot of lawyers hit a brick wall when they discover that anything foreign is involved. To press a suit successfully, a plaintiff has to overcome so many barriers, with no certainty of success, that frivolous suits will be abandoned while the playing field is leveled for serious actions. Settlements will be reasonable instead of ridiculous.

Despite their advantages, Cook Islands APTs aren't likely to become as ubiquitous as VCRs. The price tag is too high, and shopping around for discounts isn't recommended: You want a lawyer who knows how the game is played.

Typically, the process starts by creating a family limited partnership (see Chapter 27). Mom and/or Pop might control a 1 percent general-partnership interest, as well as a 99 percent limited-partnership interest. Then, the most tempting, most liquid personal assets are transferred into this partnership, behind a protective barrier.

So far, so good. But you're still subject to the vagaries of the U.S. judicial process. For belt-and-suspenders safety, the 99 percent limited-partnership interest (regardless of ownership) can be transferred to an offshore APT. Transferred *on paper*, at least. Your brokerage account, for example, still stays in New York or Dallas or wherever.

You may have a hard time convincing a court that the rental condo you own near Seattle is held in the Cook Islands, but you can borrow against your equity, and move the cash into the trust. In case of an adverse decision, the trustee may be able to move trust assets to Zurich or London. With today's technology, transactions with foreign countries are no more difficult than conducting business from one state to another.

For creating the limited partership and the APT, you'll probably pay a lawyer around $15,000, plus another couple of thousand a year to compensate the local trustee. That's expensive, but it's worth more for a really good job—you certainly don't want to spend thousands on a trust, only to have the whole process disregarded because your lawyer screwed up.

So far, relatively few law firms specialize in creating offshore APTs, but a number of major firms are in fact showing interest. And savvy lawyers will know the ins and outs: For example, you want a local trustee with *no* U.S. connections, but you also want the trust documents drawn up so he or she can't act (i.e., take your money) without your consent. Often you, the trust creator, can act as "protector," a watchdog with the power to veto distribution decisions and replace trustees.

Offshore trusts *won't* provide a tax haven—they're designed to be tax-neutral. And don't expect them to solve all of life's little problems. For example, you shouldn't set up a trust to avoid a $5,000 dispute with a landlord. Smart people don't swat flies with a sledgehammer.

When do you *need* a sledgehammer? When you're marrying late in life and don't want to discuss a prenuptial agreement with your spouse-to-be. When you've sold your business and don't want the buyer to come after the proceeds a few years later, should profits be disappointing. When you want to cut professional-liability insurance coverage, or even "go bare." When you want to protect assets while making sure they avoid probate.

In general, offshore APTs make sense for people with over $500,000 in personal wealth to protect. The more you're worth, and the greater the hazards you face, the more an APT can make sense. However, your legal position probably will be *stronger* if you keep some money in your *own* name, *within* reach of creditors, rather than move everything overseas.

SUMMING UP

• For extra asset protection, you can use an offshore trust.
• Typically, you set up a family limited partnership to hold assets, then transfer the limited-partnership interest into an offshore trust.
• Several jurisdictions have adopted laws to encourage asset protection.
• In the Cook Islands (for example), judgments by U.S. courts aren't automatically recognized, so some plaintiffs may have to start over.

• With an asset-protection trust in place, claimants may be willing to settle for minor amounts, or not bother at all to bring suits.

• Even with all this protection in place, you may still be able to keep your assets in the United States and merely shift title offshore.

• On the down side, offshore trusts are expensive to establish and maintain, and may not be able to protect assets if creditors (or potential creditors) already are in place.

30

Super Savers

Preserve Assets for Your Children and Grandchildren

So far, we've shown you how to protect your own assets from lawsuits and divorce actions, as well as from estate taxes. You may want to go one step further and protect assets for your children and grandchildren as well. To do so, you can use a special "Wealth Trust" (a trademarked term), also called a "Super Trust" or "Mega Trust." All these names are for generation-skipping dynasty trusts with a great deal of flexibility.

Wealth Trusts are irrevocable living trusts, as we saw in Chapter 28. Unlike most trusts, though, they are designed to stay in force for *three generations*. That is, after your death, the trust will continue to exist during the lifetime of your children and their children. After the *last* of your grandchildren dies, the trust terminates—and *then* the assets will be distributed to your *great-grandchildren*.

As you can see, a Wealth Trust can stay in effect for many decades. For all this time, the assets in the trust are protected—they belong to the trust, *not* to you, your children, or your grandchildren. Thus, creditors can't get at those assets, nor can divorcing spouses or anyone bringing a lawsuit. The assets will be genuinely safe for your family.

Even though the assets aren't owned by your family, they *will* be available *if needed*. The usual practice is to name your child or children as trustee(s), with grandchildren as cotrustees or successor trustees (you, as creator, usually can't be the trustee for a Wealth Trust, except in special circumstances). Children and grandchildren also can be beneficiaries. Then, if an emergency comes up, the trustee can distribute or lend trust funds to the beneficiaries.

Therefore, money in the trust will be available for education, health care, business start-ups, and other situations where heavy funding is needed. If you personally face a critical need for cash, the money can be made available to you through your *family* members.

From the Jaws of the Tax Collector

A Wealth Trust also protects wealth by avoiding estate tax for two or three generations. A dollar subjected to the top estate-tax rate—55 percent—for two generations is reduced to around 20 cents. After three estate-tax bites, only 10 cents will be left. By putting assets into a long-lived Wealth Trust, out of the reach of the estate tax, the *entire dollar* is preserved and allowed to grow.

However (here it comes), there's a special *generation-skipping tax* that's meant to *prevent* such tax avoidance. As a result, you're limited as to how much you can contribute to a Wealth Trust—$1 million per donor, $2 million per married couple. Excess amounts are subject to the generation-skipping tax, levied at 55 percent.

Thus, amounts up to $1 million or $2 million can be transferred to a Wealth Trust, over a period of years. That's the *basic funding* of the trust, but there is no limit on the *growth* of this seed money. Once you move money into the trust, the trustees can invest any way they wish. In practice, three modes of investment are most common:

1. *Municipal bonds.* The interest will be tax-exempt and can be reinvested in still more tax-exempt securities. Thus the trust fund will grow, and not be diminished by income tax.

2. *Growth stocks.* Typically, growth stocks pay little or no dividends, so little or no tax will be payable each year. Under professional management, growth stocks can be expected to generate extremely high

returns over the decades during which the Wealth Trust will be in force.

3. *Life insurance.* Money going into the fund can be used to buy life insurance on yourself, your spouse, or both. When the insured individuals die, the trust will collect the proceeds, *tax-free.*

Which way works best? If the trust creators die soon after establishing the trust, life insurance will prove to have been the better use of trust funds. If the creators live for twenty, twenty-five, or more years, the trust likely will come out ahead with stocks and bonds.

In truth, no one knows when either you or your spouse will die. Therefore, you might want to diversify your trust funds among stocks, bonds, and life insurance. Your fund will be substantial no matter *when* its creators pass on.

How substantial? Suppose you and your spouse set up a trust with three children as beneficiaries. Under current law, you can give up to $60,000 per year to the trust ($20,000 joint gift-tax exclusion times three beneficiaries) with *no* tax consequences.

Over twenty years, you can contribute $1.2 million to the trust— well below the $2 million limit for the generation-skipping tax. Thanks to stock-market growth, reinvested bond interest, and life-insurance proceeds, your Wealth Trust could accumulate $2 million, $3 million, or more, after-tax. That money will be available for your children and grandchildren.

Also, you might want to transfer real estate—a house or a condo— into a Wealth Trust. A beneficiary would be able to use the real estate without actually owning it. Thus, the house or condo would not be subject to judgments or divorce settlements. Moreover, a valued home can stay in your family for decades without generating an estate tax as it passes from generation to generation.

Subdivide and Conquer

Wealth Trusts can be tailored to suit your individual circumstances. You might, for example, provide for the trust to divide into *new* trusts, one for each of your children, after the death of yourself and your spouse. Each of the new trusts can be created by you, in advance, with the trustees and beneficiaries you think most suitable. You even can provide for these new trusts to divide into still *more* trusts, for your individual grandchildren, after the deaths of your children. If you have a great deal of confidence in one of your children or grand-children, you can name him or her as a trustee with a *special power of appointment*—the option to treat various beneficiaries in different ways, according to their circumstances.

The Wealth Trust can be combined with other strategies. You might, for example, create a family limited partnership (Chapter 27) and transfer assets to a Wealth Trust, making the trust a limited part-ner. This will give you an extra layer of asset protection.

Thanks to some quirks in the tax code, you can sell assets to your Wealth Trust for a discount from their true value. (That's because you, as general partner, control all the limited-partnership assets.) The Wealth Trust could buy assets from you on an installment basis, effectively paying you with a note and making interest-only payments for many years. In the meantime, Wealth Trust assets can be invested in stocks, bonds, or life insurance, wherein they can grow, protected from creditors and estate taxes.

You also can use a Wealth Trust as an asset-protection-plus-private-pension plan for yourself, a retirement fund that's not subject to all the restrictions of ERISA, the federal pension law. In that case, as-suming you're the spouse with most of the income and the assets, you could transfer substantial assets to your spouse. (Transfers between spouses *won't* trigger a gift tax, no matter *how* large.) Then your spouse could establish a Wealth Trust, naming you as the initial trus-tee and a beneficiary. If life insurance is used for funding, the policy would cover your spouse's life.

Again, the trust will be structured with the idea that it will serve three generations. However, if you need money for yourself, you will have access to it—as both trustee and beneficiary. This money should be the last money you ever touch, because you intend it to provide for your children and grandchildren. But it's there, in case of emer-gency—and it will stay out of the reach of ordinary creditors, as well as of malpractice claimants. No one except your own family can touch those funds.

SUMMING UP

• Irrevocable trusts designed to serve your children and grandchil-dren can provide long-term asset protection.
• Wealth Trust trustees typically will be your children and grand-children, who may have access to trust funds if necessary.

- Because of tax laws, no more than $1 million per person can be contributed to a Wealth Trust, but there is no limit as to how much the money can grow.
- Trust funds may be allocated among growth stocks, municipal bonds, and life insurance for purposes of safety and wealth-building.
- For an extra layer of asset protection, without giving up control of the assets, you can establish a family limited partnership and use a Wealth Trust to hold assets, as a limited partner.
- By having your spouse establish the trust and name you as trustee as well as a beneficiary, you can use a Wealth Trust as a private pension plan.

Part VIII

Splitting Without Getting Fractured

31

His and Hers

Prenuptial Agreements Are for Everyone—Not Just Donald and Ivana

If you're addicted to reruns of "Cheers," you've probably seen the episode in which Frasier suggests that money comes before marriage. He tells Lilith they have an appointment to draw up a prenuptial agreement, she freezes him with a look, and he goes whimpering after her, promising to forget the whole sordid business.

Fast-forward a couple of seasons. Frasier and Lilith split, and he departs for another life in another venue. But who gets what? Who gets the condo, the cars, the pension funds, the savings? On TV, those questions aren't even raised, much less answered.

In real life, though, those questions *must* be answered, down to the last penny. Often that's what the divorce lawyers spar about—at great length and expense to *both* parties. If you've been in a "bad" marriage, you may walk away with very little left after your ex-spouse and both lawyers take their shares.

Long Division

Indeed, determining each party's "share" is the hard part. Virtually every state recognizes a legal tenet, known as *marital property*, requiring that assets acquired during a marriage be divided equitably in a divorce. But which property was acquired during the marriage, and what's an equitable division thereof? Deciding on those questions is, by and large, what keeps divorce lawyers in business—and fancy trappings.

This sort of grand mess is why prenuptial agreements make sense, despite what you might see on TV. A "prenup" is a document that spells out what's yours and what's your spouse's, in case of a divorce. (Often a prenup will cover asset division at death, *too*.)

A typical prenup will spell out the property that each party brings into the marriage, stating that such belongings will remain separate—as will any gains from reinvestment. Property acquired *during* the marriage will be considered *joint* property, subject to division. In the event of divorce, the wealthier spouse might agree to pay the other spouse a certain income after (say) three years, and a greater income after five years. These promised incomes might be fixed figures ($20,000 per year or $30,000 per year), or expressed as a percentage of the wealthier spouse's income.

Take the case of Steve G., who owned a small computer company when he got married in the mid-1980s. When he and his wife divorced in the 1990s, that company was worth several million dollars. According to their prenuptial agreement, Steve was entitled to keep the company, in case of a divorce. A court upheld his agreement, and he was able to hold on to his entire company.

Even though Steve had to give up *other* assets, he was able to keep his company alive—which might not have been the case without a prenup. If a sizable portion of the company had gone to his wife, as part of a property settlement, Steve would have had a major coshareholder who didn't know the business, and also might have been hostile. She could even have sold her share to a competitor, or some other adverse party.

In addition to middle-aged people concerned about asset protection in case of divorce, elderly people also are prenup candidates. People aged sixty-five or older who are getting married after being widowed or divorced may have assets from their previous marriage(s), and children to whom they want to leave those assets. However, many states give residents an *automatic* right to a substantial share (e,g., 30 percent in Florida) of a spouse's estate, and perhaps lifetime use of the marital residence as well! With a prenuptial agreement, however, both spouses can waive those rights, thus ensuring that their assets will pass to their children.

Not a Penny More

It is clear that prenuptial agreements are important for anyone who comes into a marriage with assets. However, for prenups to stand up in the future, care must be taken *when they're drawn up*. Some lawyers say that over half of all prenups are disregarded.

A well-drawn prenup, though, *will* be recognized. Even in the highly publicized Donald and Ivana Trump divorce, "Mrs. Trump eventually received precisely what was provided in the prenuptial agreement," attorney Raoul Lionel Felder asserted to the *New York Times*.

What's the key to a solid prenup? You need to play fair with your future spouse. Beyond that, the longer the time between the signing of the prenuptial agreement and the wedding, the better. If you wait until the night before the wedding, when the out-of-town guests have arrived and the reception is all arranged, then shove a prenup under your spouse's nose, it probably won't be considered valid later on, should it be contested. Because if the question of its validity eventually arises, a court likely will say that you obtained it by coercion.

Even if you go to a lawyer two weeks before the wedding and say you want a prenuptial agreement drawn up, an *honest* lawyer won't do that, even if only because there's really not enough time left to do it *right*. In some cases, people in fact have to postpone the wedding in order to properly execute a prenup! There's no safe harbor, really, in terms of length of time before the ceremony—but the courts *have* indicated that the more time between the agreement and the marriage, the better.

So you should get a prenup signed well in advance of the ceremony. But *how*? Few prospective brides *or* grooms like the idea of dividing property into "yours" and "mine" as a precondition to wedded bliss.

One approach you might use is to tell your future mate that you want to make sure he or she is properly taken care of. A new estate plan is needed. (Actually, *that* will be the truth, in *most* situations). As part of this estate plan you'll need a will, a review of life insurance, powers of attorney, probably a trust or two—*and* a prenup. In other words, make a prenup part of a total plan to protect yourself, your future spouse, and your combined assets.

Both Sides Now

Whether or not a prenup is part of a complete estate plan, both sides should have their own lawyers. If your attorney handles everything, a court likely will rule that your spouse wasn't adequately represented, so a prenup will be disregarded. Some lawyers recommend that the signing of a prenup be videotaped, to show that both parties were represented, and agreed willingly. Not a bad idea.

Similarly, a prenup can't be "unconscionable." If you're fairly well-off, you can't stipulate that your spouse will get nothing, in case of a divorce. By the very fact of your marriage, you're offering your spouse a certain lifestyle. A prenup *can't* cut that lifestyle off, even after long years of the "worse" part of the marriage vow.

The main sticking point in most prenups, though, is *full disclosure*. When you enter into a prenup, you must spell out *all* your assets and liabilities. (In case of hard-to-value assets, such as a small business or real estate, be sure to get an independent appraisal.) Both spouses should comply in this regard.

Generally, each side should submit a complete financial statement, and turn it over to the other side for inspection. Your CPA or other financial adviser can look over the other party's statements, and raise any questions that seem appropriate. If you don't have personal financial statements, your tax-return file may be sufficient. It's hard to hide assets from someone who can check *that* out.

The idea is to present an accurate snapshot of your respective financial positions *before* your marriage. Then, in case of a divorce, you'll both be able to track the asset gain or loss, and come to a fair division. If you leave anything meaningful out of a prenup, your spouse might successfully charge fraud or deception, thus invalidating the agreement.

Sometimes, prenuptial disclosure can be telling. Mary S., for example, planned to marry Andy C. Mary had her own business, and so did Andy. They decided upon a prenuptial agreement, so she could keep her company and he could keep his, no matter what happened.

At first glance, Andy's business was considerably larger. However, as the prenuptial negotiations proceeded, Mary discovered that Andy's company had considerable exposure to unpaid payroll taxes—which might be his personal responsibility, along with substantial penalties. As a result, the prenuptial agreement included a clause indemnifying Mary on this issue.

Tax Tips

Taxes often are overlooked when prenuptial agreements are executed. If an agreement spells out who'll pay which expenses, you should include a provision on who'll pay taxes—and it *shouldn't* be simply based on each party's gross income.

The agreement should cover who'll pay to defend a tax audit, if necessary, and also who'll pay any assessed taxes, interest, and penalties. Some prenuptial agreements stipulate that the couple will file as "married, filing separately," so that tax problems from one spouse won't spill onto the other—even though the couple will wind up paying more tax that way.

If joint returns are to be filed, both spouses should be entitled to receive copies of the return *and* supporting documents, each year. This will avoid future problems in case of divorce negotiations, if one spouse can't get hold of necessary tax records. If the prenup calls for a property division, either at death or upon divorce, recognition should be given to the fact that some assets are "low-basis," and thus carry a greater future tax liability than do "high-basis" assets.

Sign Now, Save Later

To say the least, prenuptial agreements aren't cheap. A lawyer might charge you $750 for a *simple* prenup; but most agreements are fairly complex and cost between $3,000 and $5,000. (The price might be less, however, *if* included in a package along with a new will and some trusts.)

But even if a prenup does cost a few thousand dollars to draw up, the price may be well worth it, because a contested divorce can be far more costly, in legal fees as well as emotional strain. Without a prenuptial agreement, you may also suffer an adverse property settlement, while a solid prenup can preserve your premarital property.

There are other steps you can take to protect your assets from a divorce settlement. For example, you should keep *all* of your assets in your *own* name, even after you're married. Changing them to joint ownership can make them marital property, subject to a property settlement. Similarly, if you inherit assets during your marriage, or receive assets as gifts, title them in your own name. And keep careful records to show where your assets came from. *Whenever* you commingle assets with your spouse's, you risk losing them in case of a divorce.

Strictly Business

Even if you're *not* getting married, you need to be vigilant about both prenups and property ownership. Suppose you have partners in a business venture or investment property. If one of your co-owners dies or gets a divorce, his or her share might pass to someone with whom you're not comfortable—and the value of the business property could be seriously damaged. So if one of your business partners is getting married, insist that a prenuptial agreement be executed— at least with reference to the assets with which you're involved. (This may give him or her a good reason to raise the issue with the betrothed.)

You'll probably want a *right of first refusal*, too. That is, in case of a partner's death or divorce, you (and the other surviving owners) will want the right to buy the assets in question, at a fair price. Generally, this will be acceptable to any partner's future spouse, too: He or she would be getting cash instead of an illiquid interest in a small business, or in investment real estate.

The same logic applies when you enter into a business arrangement. Make sure you have a right of first refusal, in case of someone's unfortunate death or messy divorce. Then you won't have to worry about taking on unwanted partners in the future.

Make Sense, Not War

Suppose you haven't been prescient enough to execute a prenup before you're married. If your marriage runs into trouble, what can you do to prevent an unmitigated disaster? Well—you can always follow the standard procedure and hire an attorney. Of course, your spouse can do likewise. Tit for tat, as it were.

Be aware that a typical *middle-class* divorce proceeding takes *at least* a year to work out before a decree is granted, often at a total cost of around $50,000. If you have *really* substantial assets, the cost could go ballistic. What's more, over 50 percent of conventional divorces *don't* work the first time, so there is "postjudgment litigation," as the lawyers put it. In layman's terms, you can anticipate more legal costs and much more aggravation.

There's a *better* way! (As long as you and your spouse are on decent terms, that is.) Instead of *two* lawyers, you hire *one* mediator. The mediator helps you and your spouse work out an asset division between yourselves. And mediation can take you through the whole process in just a few months, at a bargain cost of only $2,000–$5,000. Voilà!

What's more, mediation can be more flexible than a conventional divorce, adapting to unusual circumstances. Take the case of John D., a Wall Street whiz who built up a million-dollar net worth in the 1980s. After the 1987 crash, John lost his job. Using his capital, he started up a new health-care business. But the strain turned out to be unhealthy for his marriage, so he and his wife, Jane, decided to heal themselves through divorce, if possible.

In a conventional (adversarial) divorce, Jane would have been entitled to a certain level of child support, as well as a property settlement. However, the money would have come out of John's new business, hurting its chances for success. In a few years the business could go under, and John might not have been able to keep paying child support. Instead, John and Jane used mediation. As a result, Jane accepted a lower level of child support *and* passed up a property settlement, leaving the latter money in the business. In turn, she would gradually be entitled to a greater level of child support, *plus* a share of the company if it succeeded.

You and your spouse, should you face divorce, likely would want to hire your own lawyers, if only to approve a mediated settlement. Good move! Still, if you could keep your barristers from taking over the proceedings, you'd likely find that mediation would pay off rather better for you, and less well for them. For information and help in finding mediators, call the Academy of Family Mediatiors in Portland, Oregon, 503-345-1205.

SUMMING UP

• When people who have assets—or who expect to have assets at some point—get married, steps should be taken to protect those pluses.

• A *prenuptial agreement* (prenup) can spell out what will happen to each party's assets, in case of death or divorce.

• Prenups can help middle-aged people, as well as elderly people who remarry and want to protect the children of a prior marriage.

• A typical prenup will keep each party's assets separate while stipulating that assets acquired during a marriage are subject to a fair division.

• In order for a prenuptial agreement to be valid, it should be arrived at only after ample time for mutually satisfactory negotiation.

• Both sides should have their own lawyers, and fully disclose all their assets in order to draw up a valid prenuptial agreement.

• Either an attorney or a CPA should point out all the tax ramifications of a prenuptial agreement.

• After a marriage, it's easier to protect your property if you keep it in your own name, rather than attached to joint ownership.

• If you do find yourself in a divorce situation, mediation is faster and cheaper than the typical adversarial proceeding.

32

Send the Bill to the IRS

Structure a Divorce Agreement So Both Sides Come Out Ahead

If you ever find yourself in the midst of a divorce, you'll face an overwhelming array of emotional, familial, and financial problems. (If you've been *through* one, just ride with this.) But don't forget the IRS—because divorce, like death, has tax consequences. With careful planning, you not only can reduce the tax bite, but you also can get the IRS to subsidize your family!

The prime tax issue in divorce is whether or not alimony is paid:

• Alimony payments *are* deductible, and the recipient thereof *must* admit to taxable income.

• Child-support payments and property settlements *are not* deductible, and the recipient thereof *does not* admit to any taxable income.

Naturally, if you're the spouse who'll be making the payments, you'd like to have them characterized as *deductible* alimony. Just as naturally, the spouse who'll be receiving the payments wants *untaxed* property settlements and child support.

If you, the payer, are in a relatively high tax bracket (28 percent +), and your spouse stands to be in a 15 percent bracket (because there will be little or no other income for him or her), you can play a win-win game. In essence, you can increase the payment amounts by 20 percent or more, characterizing them as alimony rather than child support.

For example: Suppose you were to pay your spouse $2,000 a month in *child support*. You'd be out $2,000 and he or she would be ahead by $2,000. Instead, you pay $2,500 a month in *alimony*. Your spouse, in a 15 percent tax bracket, winds up with $2,125 a month. Assuming you're in a 40 percent tax bracket (counting state and local income taxes), your $2,500 deduction saves you $1,000 in taxes each month, bringing your net outlay down to $1,500. You *both* wind up ahead, and the IRS effectively subsidizes your divorce: You pay $1,500 a month, *after-tax*, and your spouse *nets* $2,125!

Of course, such magical results are not all that easy to achieve. Behind the magic is the reality that for a payment to qualify as deductible alimony, the following conditions must be met:

• Payments must be made in *cash*. There's little leeway here beyond checks and money orders.

• Payments must be made to or "on behalf of" the recipient. (At the written request of the recipient, payments can be made *directly* for rent, taxes, school tuition, home mortgages, or life-insurance premiums.)

• Payments must be *required* by a written divorce or separation agreement.

• Payments may *not* be designated as nondeductible or nonincludible in these agreements.

• The payor and the recipient *can't* live in the same household.

• The payments *must* terminate at the recipient's death.

• The payments *must not* be in the nature of child support.

Child Supporters

If payments terminate at the recipient's death, the children may be unprotected. So there should be other financial assets available for the children, or at least strong family support (including financial help) that you can rely upon. On the other hand, the payments may not need to go on at such high levels after the children are grown and the need is reduced. Some courts have okayed *finite-term alimony payments* when the term hasn't been directly tied to dependents' needs.

Today, many divorcing couples limit alimony payments to the amount of time it will take for the homemaker spouse to get back into the work force—generally from two to five years. If there are dependent children this might take longer—perhaps from six to ten years. Suppose you have two teenagers. You might want to pay $2,000 per month for as long as both kids are dependents, and $1,000 per month after the first child is on his or her own.

However, if you structure alimony payments in this manner, there are certain rules you must follow: You can't, for example, have the phaseout dates within six months of the children's reaching of age twenty-one, for example. Therefore, you need to work with a savvy divorce lawyer, to avoid tax traps.

Whether you're paying alimony or child support, you're often required to carry life insurance. That way, if you die before you've made all the agreed-upon payments, your ex-spouse will receive the insurance proceeds to make up the shortfall. (Generally, you'll buy term insurance, letting the insurance lapse after the obligation ends.)

But look what happens if you simply pay the premiums on that policy: If you die while the policy is in force, the proceeds will be included in your taxable estate, and your heirs (perhaps a second spouse) may owe an estate tax while your ex-spouse gets the insurance proceeds, tax-free!

To avoid this unhappy scenario, set up an irrevocable life-insurance trust, to hold the policy *outside of* your estate. Or, insist that your ex-spouse own the policy, using money you give to him or her to pay the premiums.

Property Rights and Wrongs

Tax considerations enter into property settlements, too. Suppose you have assets worth $300,000. In a property settlement, you agree to transfer $150,000. The question is: which $150,000?

In a property settlement, the recipient inherits the *cost basis*. Thus, if you transfer $150,000 worth of stock for which you've paid

$100,000, the built-in $50,000 capital-gain tax obligation goes with it. The same principle applies if you transfer your interest in the family home, or other real estate.

Often it's better to transfer assets (e.g., income-paying stocks and bonds) that are not likely to be sold. If your spouse holds on until his or her death, the capital gain will be wiped out. But if you transfer $150,000 worth of growth stocks, and your spouse sells those stocks to reinvest in interest-paying bonds, he or she will immediately incur a $50,000 capital gain. So, if a sale and reinvestment are inevitable, it's best to transfer *high-basis* assets, and to have the *lower-bracket* spouse bear the tax.

Of course, if you're strictly looking out for Number One, you're better off giving your spouse your *low-basis* assets and retaining the high-basis assets for yourself.

Finally, if you have dependent children, their personal exemptions may be negotiable. Taxpayers with adjusted gross income of over $110,000 lose the benefit of these exemptions (pegged at $2,450 per exemption in 1994). So, if you'll be in this situation, consider allocating these exemptions to your spouse, on IRS Form 8332, in return for concessions elsewhere in the divorce negotiations.

SUMMING UP

• In a divorce settlement, alimony is a taxable event—deductible for the payor and taxable for the recipient—whereas child support and property settlements aren't taxable.

• If one divorcing spouse will be in a much higher bracket than the other, both sides can come out ahead by focusing on alimony in the financial settlement.

• Although alimony may be necessary while the children still are dependents, it's increasingly common for alimony to stop after a certain time period—anywhere from two to ten years.

• If you have to carry term life insurance as part of a divorce settlement, keep the proceeds out of your taxable estate by holding the policy in an irrevocable trust, or have your ex-spouse hold it.

• When you transfer assets as part of a property settlement, giving away highly appreciated assets can reduce your future tax obligations.

Part IX

Exit Laughing

33

You Don't Need to Be a Millionaire . . .

to Have an Estate Plan

Your estate is, in essence, your life's work. If you have managed to acquire any assets, and you protect them against the perils we've described previously, you'll *have* an estate. To truly protect what's yours, however, you'll need to pass those assets on to your family—and to do that with a minimum of cost and confusion. You'll therefore need an *estate plan*.

When you think of estate planning, you may think of Rockefellers and Fords and DuPonts, with batteries of attorneys laboring to save millions in taxes through complex trust arrangements. But estate planning *isn't* just for the super-rich. If you have a house, a bank account, or a pension plan, you need an estate plan in order to ensure that those assets are transferred according to your wishes.

Will Power

The *sine qua non* of an estate plan is a will, since if you *don't* have a will, you *can't* have an estate plan. Your will should be drawn up by an attorney, and witnessed by unrelated parties. Make copies, but sign only the *original*, to avoid possible technical problems. (Your family needs to know the location of the original, which should be kept in a fireproof office safe or filing cabinet.)

Leaving your will in a bank safe-deposit box probably is *not* a good idea. In many states, your bank vault will be sealed right after your death, so that all the assets can be tallied—and possibly taxed. Thus, there may be delays in getting your will and distributing your assets according to its terms.

Don't worry too much about the form or contents of your will—that's your lawyer's job. Spell out for your lawyer as best you can how you want your assets distributed. Just be sure you name beneficiaries in full, and describe assets as completely as possible. Don't say, "the contents of my office desk," for instance—because you don't know what will be in there at the time of your death.

You probably won't want to list in your will every dish and desk ornament you own, so it's a good idea to have a separate *letter of instruction* as a supplement. As you acquire or dispose of possessions, this document can be updated.

You can explain your desired funeral and burial arrangements in your will. If you have minor children, you should name guardians, in case you and your spouse (if any) should die together. These guardians will be substitute parents, so you should name people most likely to fill that role. Cousins or siblings who have kids the same age as yours are good candidates.

Many people use trusts to hold title to their assets. However, it's unlikely that all of your assets, from your antiques to your zebra fish, will be owned by a trust. A *"pour over" will* can cover assets *not* held in trust, pouring them into a trust at your death, if desired.

Your will needs to be reviewed at least once every three years—perhaps more often. Federal tax laws change so rapidly that you should have an expert check your will frequently. Changes in family circumstances (births, deaths, marriages, divorces) are likely occasions for review. If you move to a different state, revise your will—because state laws differ. Depending on the magnitude of the change, you may need either a complete rewrite or just a simple addition called a *codicil*.

Courting Trouble

What if you die without a valid will in place? You'll be classified "intestate" and your property will be divided up according to a state formula, not your wishes.

For example, Solomon K. won $5 million in the New York State lottery in 1987. The fifty-four-year-old janitor became an ex-janitor and announced he'd take care of his family. He promised to help fix a sister's leaky roof; he told his handicapped niece he would buy her a van; other family members were told they would share in this good fortune.

Unfortunately, Solomon was killed in a car accident in 1988. Even worse (for them, at least), his family soon discovered that he had never made a will. For years, his two children and three surviving sisters and the Surrogate's Court of New York struggled to arrive at a fair distribution of Solomon's estate.

Much the same thing—though probably on a smaller scale—will happen to *your* "heirs" if *you* die without a will. Your family's fortunes will be in the hands of a court. No tax-reduction strategies will be pursued, and court-appointed outsiders may wind up telling your family what to do.

In some states, half of your assets will go to your children, not to your surviving spouse. Minor children may become wards of the state, so your surviving spouse will have to account to a court for every penny spent on their behalf. When your children come of age (eighteen, in many states), they may be entitled to *all* of their share of the assets, *no* strings attached. And if they're dissatisfied with the way your spouse has handled their assets, they can sue!

If your spouse remarries, the new husband or wife may be able to gain control over the assets you left to your spouse, with no guarantee they'll *ever* go to your children. And other family members, such as parents or siblings, may be cut out altogether. In essence, dying without a will deprives you of any say in the distribution of your estate.

Very likely, *none* of all this is what you have in mind for an estate plan. Therefore, it's well worth spending time and money on a professionally created will.

Probate's Not Great

In your will you'll also name an *executor* (sometimes called a *personal representative*). After your death, it's the executor's responsibility to handle all the paperwork and make sure the assets are distributed. Your executor needn't be a lawyer; your spouse, or even a grown child of yours, probably could fill that role. Patience and a sense of responsibility are the main requirements. Just make sure you get the executor's consent before naming him or her in the will.

After your death, many of your assets will go through *probate*—that's the process of "proving" your will and transferring your assets to your heirs. Depending on your state, the costs of probate might be as much as 7 percent of your assets. If you have a $200,000 brokerage account, transferring it to your heirs could cost your family $14,000 in attorney fees and court costs.

In some states, an estate can take two years to clear probate. *All* probate proceedings are part of the public record, so *anyone* can learn about your holdings, the debts you've incurred, and so on.

On the bright side, many types of assets are automatically exempt from probate: property that is held jointly, life-insurance proceeds (as long as you name a beneficiary who isn't a minor), retirement-plan assets (ditto), and certain bank accounts with "payable on death," or POD, provisions. If most of your assets fall into those categories, probate will be a nuisance—but at least not a disaster.

However, if you hold a significant amount of real estate in your own name, or an investment portfolio, or a closely held business, your family will have to contend with a great deal of nuisance in dealing with probate.

Out of Your Hands

Another way to avoid probate is to establish a *living trust*. In fact *any* trust established while you're alive is a living trust. Many people whose main goal is the avoidance of probate use *revocable* living trusts, which can be revoked or annulled by the trust creator.

Typically, the creator of the trust acts as trustee *and* as beneficiary. The ownership of your assets can be transferred to the trust. You still remain in control, as trustee, and you receive the trust income, as beneficiary. In case you change your mind, you can revoke the trust and take the assets back under your own name.

Every state recognizes *these* trusts, so you *don't* need to rewrite one if you move. Some updating may be necessary, as your personal situation changes, but revocable living trusts aren't hard to modify. You can amend the trust with only your signature, and witnesses aren't necessary.

Assuming you're pleased with the trust, you'll hold the assets in there until your death. Then, the revocable trust automatically becomes an *irrevocable* trust. A successor trustee, whom you have named, will distribute the trust assets according to the instructions you set out in your trust documents. Therefore, the trust assets pass to your heirs *without* going through probate. There's no time lag, and no public record.

This technique is versatile enough so that you can set up additional trusts, for special purposes, using assets from your living trust. These trusts are particularly helpful if you own real estate in more than one state, because your property doesn't have to go through probate in each of them.

Time and Money

There are, however, *disadvantages* to living trusts. For example, the money your family will save by going through probate will be offset by the money you pay to set up and administer the trust. Plus, the trust will work only if you take the time and effort to retitle your assets and change ownership.

Setting up a revocable living trust *won't* cut your taxes. You'll still owe tax on income from trust assets, which still will be included in your taxable estate. Indeed, if you want to make gifts in order to reduce your taxable estate, you probably shouldn't make them directly from the trust. To avoid IRS displeasure, it's better to take assets from the trust back into your own name, then give them away in order to reduce your estate.

Do revocable living trusts make sense? A lot depends on the shape of your portfolio. Several types of assets avoid probate: Jointly owned assets go directly to the surviving owners, while insurance proceeds and retirement plans (and some bank accounts) go directly to beneficiaries. If your assets chiefly fall into these categories, you won't have much probate to avoid.

So don't rush into a revocable living trust. Check around to see if your state has a reputation for being fast and cheap, or slow and costly, when it comes to probate. Ask your lawyer what the costs will be *before* you decide to make a commitment.

SUMMING UP

• Regardless of whether your assets are large or small, you should have a will.

• A bona fide will, drawn up by an experienced lawyer, can ensure that your assets will be distributed according to your wishes.

• If you die *without* a will, the distribution of your property will be determined by state law, and the results probably will not be what you would have wanted.

• Because you won't be able to mention all of your assets in your will, a separate *letter of instruction* should be used to specify how your possessions ought to be distributed.

• If you have minor children, you should name *guardians* in your will, in case you and your spouse both die.

• You should name an *executor*, who'll administer your estate and see to it that your property is transferred.

• A diligent family member can serve as executor, but you might want to name a financial institution as coexecutor if your estate is sizable.

• Assets left via a will go through *probate*, which can be expensive, time-consuming, and subject to public scrutiny.

• If you transfer assets to a *living trust*, they'll bypass probate after your death.

• Living trusts are worthwhile *when* you have substantial assets that would be subject to probate, and *if* you retitle those assets to the trust.

34

Life Goes On

What You Really Need to Know About Life Insurance

You need to protect your family as well as your physical possessions. From a financial point of view, if you're the main source of income in your household, you need to provide for your family in case you die while you still have dependents. To supply this protection, you need to buy enough life insurance to take care of your family—but to protect your assets, you should buy no more than what's truly necessary.

To determine the right amount of life insurance to carry, you and your spouse (presuming there is one) must decide how much money would be needed to cover basic living expenses for your immediate family in case of your sudden death. Let's say the number is $3,000 per month.

Next, estimate how much income your family could reasonably expect only from your spouse's job, investment income, Social Security benefits, etc. Suppose that number, after-tax, will be $1,800 per month. The shortfall would be $1,200 per month.

Then, determine which assets could be converted to income production. For example, your family might sell a vacation home and invest the proceeds in corporate bonds. Say they'd realize $120,000 and earn a 5 percent return, after-tax. That would be $6,000 per year, or $500 a month. *Now* the shortfall would be down to $700 monthly.

Estimated monthly expenses	$3,000
(Minus) expected monthly income	(1,800)
(Minus) income from other assets	(500)
Monthly shortfall	$ 700

If your shortfall *is* $700 per month, that would be $8,400 in just one year—quite a sum. Assuming a 5 percent return, after-tax, you'd then need $168,000 worth of life insurance. (You might buy $200,000 worth, just to be safe.)

Your $3,000 monthly budget probably wouldn't include money to put your kids through college. (Four years at a *top* private school now costs about $100,000.) If you plan to send your children to such a place, increase your total life insurance by $100,000 for *each* child. If you *don't* expect them to attend such a pricey college, increase life insurance by $50,000 apiece.

Every couple of years, go over your life-insurance needs. If your family has gradually gotten used to a richer lifestyle, you might increase the amount. On the other hand, after you've put your kids through college and you have a substantial amount in a retirement fund, you might well reduce your coverage—or eliminate it altogether.

One Year at a Time

How can you afford to buy up to $400,000 worth of life insurance? The least expensive type of life insurance is *term* insurance. You pay only so much in premiums for just so much insurance protection, for a stated time period (usually one year). After that, you pay another—and probably higher—premium for another term. Generally, premiums increase as you grow older. (You can buy term insurance where the premium will stay level for a number of years, but you're essentially shifting later costs to earlier years.)

You probably will be best served by buying *low-cost* term insurance. Be sure you buy *guaranteed renewable* term, because then the insurer can't cancel your coverage, as long as you pay the premiums. Also, you won't need to take any more physical exams, once you've passed the first one.

Term insurance *is* "pure" insurance, but be reminded that it comes with the catch we mentioned: The *older* you get, the *more* it may cost. If you're still carrying life insurance in your sixties and seventies, you're probably paying *huge* premiums for term insurance.

As an alternative, you can buy *permanent* life insurance. Here, you pay a *fixed* premium per year—the same one, year after year. However, permanent life is much more expensive than term in the *early* years. Depending upon your age, the same coverage you can buy for $300 per year for term insurance might cost up to $3,000 annually for permanent life!

Why pay $3,000 instead of $300? Because you get investment buildup and tax shelter. Most of your permanent life premium goes into an investment account, the "cash value," where it can compound, free of income tax. What's more, you can take out policy loans and withdrawals from the cash value (up to certain limits) without paying taxes. And you don't have to pay interest on any loans. However, outstanding policy loans and loan interest *will* be subtracted from the amount your beneficiaries receive upon your death.

Cash-value life insurance works only if you stay in for many years. Your first premium payments go largely to the sales agent, and there usually are a variety of early withdrawal penalties. If you need to get your cash back after only a year or two, you may wind up with even less than you paid in. Also, when you surrender a policy, you'll owe tax on all the investment income you've sheltered inside the policy. Buy permanent life *only* if you plan to hold the policy for at least fifteen years.

In for the Long Haul

When does *permanent* life insurance make better sense than term coverage? When your income is so great that you can pay the premiums without financial strain, and you welcome the tax shelter for investment income. Also, if you start a family late in life, you may prefer permanent life rather than term insurance because term premiums become relatively so expensive. Permanent life also makes sense for middle-aged and elderly people who have amassed a *great* deal of wealth. Your family may well need its proceeds to pay an estate tax.

Term insurance becomes extremely expensive as you go into your seventies and eighties, the time in many people's lives when they first realize how much they'll owe in estate taxes. A $500,000 policy, which might have cost you only $500 per year while you were in your thirties, might increase to $10,000 or $20,000 or more. (Some insurers won't even sell term insurance to the elderly.) Suppose the premium goes so high that you skip a payment—even your first ever. Despite your having carried the policy for years, it will lapse when you do that— and your heirs won't get a cent of the prospective insurance proceeds.

Obviously permanent life insurance makes the best sense when you're insuring to pay an estate tax. Unless you lose or spend most of your wealth, you'll *never* outgrow your need for cash to pay estate tax.

Some agents may offer you a policy which, to bring down the initial cost, mixes term with permanent insurance. That may be a good initial strategy, but (again) term insurance becomes tremendously expensive as you grow older. Find out how much term is included in the mix, and how high future premiums may go, before you consider buying.

Vanishing Acts

Actually, few people buy permanent life insurance with the idea that they'll pay premiums every year until they die. Suppose you want to buy a $500,000 policy. Your agent likely will suggest that instead of paying say $7,000 per year for the rest of your life, that you pay $10,000 per year. After perhaps eleven years, your obligation to pay premiums will "vanish."

The more money you pay up front, the greater the cash value will be. The cash value may even generate enough earnings to keep paying premiums, through the years, after *you* stop paying.

To back up the sales pitch, the agent likely will show you an "illustration," a computerized printout showing eleven years of $10,000 payments, a buildup of cash value, and a death benefit of around $500,000. It's hard not to be impressed by the columns of numbers.

Remember, though, that *all* permanent life insurance is a guessing game. An illustration merely puts those guesses on paper. There is *no way* the insurer can know how much it will earn, year after year, on the $110,000 you pay in. There is *no way* they can know things

such as company expenses and mortality rates (how many policyholders will die each year).

Naturally, some insurers are more aggressive than others in their
projections. They might predict a 10 percent compound growth on
your invested premiums, while others project 7 percent. And they can
make similarly optimistic assumptions about other factors, too. These
companies' illustrations will of course tend to show higher cash values
and lower premium payments for any given level of insurance than
will the more reality-oriented ones.

If you buy a policy based on flawed projections, you might find that
your cash value isn't growing as fast as expected, and thus also isn't
generating enough income to pay future premiums. You may find that
your premium vanishes not after just eleven years, but after an
agonizing twenty. Instead of buying a $500,000 policy for $110,000,
you might wind up paying over $200,000!

To avoid these pitfalls, you need to find out which assumptions are
being used in the illustration. Ask about the *assumed rate for investment earnings*. If it seems unreasonable, ask to have the illustration
rerun at a lower, more realistic rate. Even more important: Buy from
established insurers. Look for a company with excellent ratings from
two or more independent agencies (*at least* A + from A. M. Best; AA
from Standard & Poor's or Moody's; and B from Weiss Research),
and at least fifty years of experience in the business.

Keeping Your Options Open

The most basic type of permanent life insurance is called *whole life*.
An increasingly popular variation is *universal life*. The key difference
is that with the latter you can vary your premiums from year to year.
You can reduce your payments if you're short of cash, or you can
increase payments as your income grows. As your payments vary, your
death benefit and cash value will vary accordingly. Obviously the more
you pay, the more coverage you'll have.

Yet another type of permanent life insurance is *variable life*. Your
premium payments can be directed into various investment accounts—mainly mutual funds. Most variable life policies offer stock
funds, bond funds, and money-market funds, while some also include
real estate, international investments, zero-coupon bonds, and other
categories.

Your death benefit and your cash value will reflect the success of the investments you choose. You may even lose money! However, the insurance company is required to guarantee a *minimum death benefit*: Your beneficiaries will receive *at least* as much as the amount you paid in premiums.

Generally, variable life insurance is suitable for younger investors— those with a long time to invest. Only those with sizable incomes and net worth should consider this coverage, because of the risks. If you're in this fortunate category, put most of your premiums into stock funds—and hold on for the long term.

For flexibility plus the chance for a large buildup, you can buy *universal variable* life, which (as you may have guessed) combines the features of universal life *and* variable life. However, if your main concern is simply insurance coverage, you may prefer to stick with plain vanilla *whole life*, which offers stronger guarantees than the variations cited.

Double Coverage

If you're married and buying life insurance for estate-planning pur- poses, you may want to buy *survivorship life*, commonly called *sec- ond-to-die* insurance. These policies insure two lives, and pay off only after *both* deaths.

Second-to-die life is increasingly popular because it's cheaper than buying policies on both spouses. The exact pricing will vary, depend- ing on the age of the insured individuals, but this kind of policy might cut your cost by 20 percent or more of the cost of buying two single- life policies. Moreover, buying a second-to-die policy means no guess- ing games about who'll die first.

No matter which spouse does die first, *most* of the estate can go to the survivor—with little or no estate tax due. When the survivor dies, the money can pass to the children. The estate tax will be due *then*, but that obligation may be covered by the insurance proceeds.

You'll see policy illustrations for second-to-die life, too. Be careful of any potentially misleading projections! Some illustrations, for ex- ample, assume that both spouses will live for 100 years. Ask what would happen if one spouse were to die soon, and the other live for many years: Will premiums shoot up?

In Sickness and in Health

No matter *what* kind of life insurance you want to buy, you'll have to pass a physical to get it. Top-rated insurance companies are *very* choosy about whom they insure (that's how they get to be on top). Nevertheless, even the best insurers cover *some* less-than-healthy individuals (they take moderate risks, in return for higher premiums).

Insurance companies base their rates on "standard" risks. These are people with no significant health problems, who can be expected to live to normal life expectancies. Some companies offer discounted rates to individuals (called "preferred" risks) in above-average health.

People with health problems are *rated*. Ratings start with Table 1, for slight problems—such as being only a little overweight. As your health problems increase, your rating goes to Table 2 (e.g., diabetes), Table 4 (uncontrolled hypertension), Table 8 (liver problems), and Table 12 (abnormal EKG), for example. Some companies have sixteen tables. Although a few conditions (AIDS, advanced cancer) do make it impossible to buy *any* life insurance, most people will find a place *somewhere* on the tables.

In some cases, your rating will be determined by occupation (e.g., police officer) rather than by health condition, because some occupations are intrinsically hazardous.

Prices vary from company to company, but you can expect to pay 25 percent above the standard price for each rating level. A policy that would cost you $1,000 in standard health might cost you $1,250 in Table 1 and $1,500 in Table 2. Therefore, it's in your interest to get as *low* a rating as possible. (Some agents are experts on *impaired-risk* insurance. If your own agent says there's a health problem, ask for a referral to an agent who specializes in impaired risks.)

Remember that ratings vary from one insurer to another. For example, insurers believe that heart attacks are caused by smoking, by high blood pressure, and by high cholesterol levels. They differ, though, on how much weight they assign to each factor. If you apply to three companies, you'll get three medical exams and three evaluations. Also, there may be significant differences in what each company charges for the same amount of life insurance.

Whenever you apply for life insurance, the company will ask for an attending physician's (AP) statement, as well as a physical exam. The AP statement is a report from your family doctor that gives an overall picture of your health. If your agent (or an impaired-risk specialist) gets the AP statement first, he or she can apply to the insurer that's best for people with hypertension, for example; or to the insurance company that's lenient with applicants who have had bypass operations. If you're in excellent health, your agent can confidently apply to companies that are best for preferred risks.

No matter what anyone tells you, *don't* lie about your health on a life-insurance application. If you conceal a condition, and that omission is exposed, your policy eventually may be cancelled. Worse, the insurer may contest the claim after your death. After a policyholder dies, an insurer may refuse to pay, citing a misleading application.

You may in fact want to defer making an application until you've lost some weight, stopped smoking, or addressed some other health problem. The better condition you're in when you take your physical, the less you'll wind up paying for life insurance. When bought for the right purpose and at the right price, life insurance offers tax advantages unmatched by any other financial vehicles.

SUMMING UP

• If you have dependents, you need life insurance to provide income in case of your unexpected death.

• To determine how much insurance to buy, project the shortfall between ongoing income and expenses after your death, and cover yourself for about twenty times what your family will need each year.

• Buy *extra* life insurance in order to pay for your children's college education.

• Initially, the *least expensive* form of life insurance is *term* insurance, which however becomes more costly as you grow older.

• *Permanent* life insurance is initially *more* expensive, but may prove to be *less* costly, than term as you grow older.

• Permanent life insurance offers tax-free buildup *and* the ability to tap that buildup, tax-free.

• In order to realize the benefits of permanent life insurance, you need to hold the policy for *at least* fifteen years.

• Although an insurance policy illustration may promise that your responsibility for paying premiums will vanish after a certain number of years, such illustrations are only projections based on assumptions that may prove inaccurate.

• For estate-planning purposes, you may want to buy relatively inexpensive *second-to-die* life insurance, which will pay off after both spouses die and the estate tax is due.

• Most people are insurable, but healthy individuals will pay lower life-insurance premiums.

35

Disinheriting the Taxman

Basic Estate-Tax Reduction Strategies

Besides protecting your assets during your lifetime, you probably want to leave behind as much as you can for your family. You certainly don't want to leave hundreds of thousands of dollars to the IRS. Unfortunately, the federal government will become one of your *principal* heirs—unless you do some tax planning.

Everyone is entitled to a $600,000 estate-tax exemption. If your estate is valued at *less* than $600,000 when you die, *no* estate tax will be due. But that doesn't mean if you have $600,000 in the bank, period. At your death, your executor will be responsible for adding up *all* of your assets, and filing a tax return thereon. The value of your house, your retirement plan, your investments, and everything else you own must be accounted for.

If the executor's total is *over* $600,000, your estate *will* owe taxes—and at a breathtakingly steep rate. The very lowest bracket is 37 percent, so if you have a $700,000 estate, you'll owe $37,000 on the excess $100,000. From there, the tax escalates to 55 percent, with a special

60 percent bracket on estates ranging in value from $10 million to $21 million.

In most cases, the estate tax will be due—in full—within nine months of your death. If cash isn't readily available, your executor may have to sell real estate, stocks, or other assets (in a hurry) to raise the money.

The Joy of Giving

If you reduce the size of your estate, you'll automatically reduce your estate's tax obligation. One strategy is to give away assets. However, there's a gift tax that's "unified" with the estate tax: In essence, whatever assets you give away reduce your estate-tax exemption. Let's look at some examples of how this strange system works (or doesn't).

Say you give away $100,000 before you die. Now, your estate-tax exemption is $500,000, *not* $600,000. And if you give away $800,000, your executor will have to pay a gift tax on the "excess" $200,000, at estate-tax rates.

Suppose you make gifts frequently, sending for instance birthday presents to your grandchildren, and anniversary presents to your children. Does every $50 check you write come out of your estate-tax exemption? No. At least not yet. In fact, under current law, anyone can make gifts of up to $10,000 each year, to *any* number of recipients, *without* reducing your gift- or estate-tax exemption. Say you have two children, plus a son- and daughter-in-law, and six grandchildren. You could give each of them up to $10,000 worth of assets per year (annually $100,000 in all), with *no* tax consequences. You wouldn't even have to fill out any gift-tax returns!

If you're married, the allowance increases to $20,000 per recipient per year, as long as your spouse formally agrees to the gifts. Given the rest of the family in the above example, you could reduce your taxable estate by up to $200,000 per year.

In addition to gifts of up to $20,000 per year, you can use the "med-ed" exclusion. That is, you can make unlimited gifts of medical payments and tuition on behalf of someone else, providing the payments are made directly to the health-care provider or school.

Give While the Giving Is Good

You also can make larger lifetime gifts, in effect using up part or all of your $600,000 lifetime exemption from gift- and estate taxes. Why should you do this? Politicians are hungry to tax the rich, and what better way than to increase estate taxes? Because of them, the $600,000 threshold may be dropped to as low as $300,000. If you act now, you may be able to make a larger tax-free gift while this shelter is still available. Also, once you give away assets, any future appreciation will be excluded from your taxable estate.

If you make gifts in order to reduce your estate tax, they should be made in cash, if at all possible, to avoid tax complications. If you have securities with a loss position (they have fallen in value since you bought them), you can sell them, take the tax loss, and then give away cash. On the other hand, giving away appreciated securities saddles the recipient with a low tax basis—and a tax obligation when the securities are sold.

When you make sizable gifts, look for assets that are likely to *appreciate* before you die. The 1990s may be an excellent time to give away real estate, for example: The current value may be low, because of depressed market conditions, and *any* recovery in real-estate prices won't increase your taxable estate. The same reasoning applies if you own shares in a small business whose earnings have been depressed.

Gifts such as real estate, and shares in a private business, need a valuation that will stand up to possible IRS scrutiny—so an independent appraisal is recommended.

Capital Gain, No Pain

Your appreciated assets should be held until you die. Under current law, at that time all your assets get a *step-up in basis*. Let's look into this a bit.

Suppose you purchased mutual-fund shares ten years ago, for $100,000. By the time of your death, those shares have appreciated in value to $300,000. Whoever inherits those shares gets a *new basis*—$300,000 instead of $100,000. If he or she sells the shares right away, for $300,000, *no* income tax will be due. The $200,000 capital gain goes untaxed! And the same is true for your home, other real estate, business interests, and any appreciated assets.

Gift and estate taxes *don't* apply when you either give or leave assets to your spouse. No matter how large, such transfers aren't taxed. You can have a $2 million estate—even a $10 million estate. If you leave everything to your spouse at your death, *no* estate tax will be due.

However, when your spouse dies, and those assets pass to your children and grandchildren, everything over $600,000 *will* be subject to an estate tax.

Trusts Are a Must

Most estate planning involves the use of trusts, in order to hold title to assets. To avoid estate and income taxes, you can transfer assets to an *irrevocable trust*, so that the assets are definitely out of your control.

Suppose, for example, you're making $10,000 annual gifts to reduce your taxable estate. Minors can't hold assets legally, so gifts to your grandchildren may have to be either in a trust or in a custodial account. Even gifts to adults might be made to a trust, if you have doubts about that adult's ability to handle money carefully. When gifts *are* made in trust, the assets can be preserved from creditors, from divorce actions, and from general squandering alike.

You may be able to make large annual gifts to a trust, free of a gift tax, if you follow the trail blazed by Maria Cristofani, a widow with two children, Frank and Lillian. She set up a trust, naming her children as *primary* beneficiaries. Their five children (Maria's grandchildren), ages two through eleven, were named *secondary* beneficiaries. If either Frank or Lillian failed to outlive Maria by 120 days, that child's children would split his or her share.

After setting up the trust, Maria transferred assets valued at $70,000 to the trust in 1984, and again in 1985. But then Maria died—and the IRS demanded back-taxes. According to the IRS, $20,000 of the annual gifts could be excluded, but the other $50,000 per year was subject to a gift tax. The Cristofani estate contended, and the Tax Court agreed, that there were seven trust beneficiaries—Frank, Lillian, and the five grandchildren. Under the terms of the trust, each beneficiary had a "Crummey" power—so called by virtue of taking the name of a landmark case.

After each contribution, the grandchildren had the legal right to withdraw assets from the trust, during a fifteen-day period, and so they had a "present interest" in the gifts. Therefore, Maria was entitled to give $10,000 per year to each of them, and the $70,000 gifts incurred no gift tax.

The court actually approved a very cozy setup. Frank and Lillian, the primary beneficiaries, also were the trustees. The secondary beneficiaries all were minors who, were they to exercise their withdrawal rights, could do so *only* through their guardians. And who were those guardians? Their parents, including Frank and Lillian. So Frank and Lillian had control over *all* the trust assets. Maria Cristofani effectively transferred $140,000 worth of assets to her two children in two years, without owing a cent of gift tax.

Thanks a $1.2 Million

Putting together the pieces outlined above, here's an estate-tax plan suitable for most families: First, make sure that you and your spouse each have at least $600,000 in assets—held outright, *not* jointly. If one spouse has significantly greater assets than the other, tax-free spousal gifts can be used to make sure each spouse has at least $600,000.

Then, each spouse should have either a will or a living trust stating that $600,000 should pass to children or grandchildren at his or her death. No matter *which* spouse dies first, $600,000 will go to future generations, tax-free, because of the estate-tax exemption. The rest should be left to the other spouse, tax-free, because it's a bequest to a spouse. Therefore, no estate tax will be due at the first death.

In the interim period following the first death, the surviving spouse can make tax-free gifts, up to the $10,000 annual limit. At the second death, when all the remaining assets are passed down, another $600,000 will be sheltered. Thus, $1.2 million (plus any assets transferred through gifts) will escape the estate tax.

This strategy calls for $600,000 to pass to your children from the first spouse to die. This may not leave the surviving spouse with enough income to live in comfort. In that case, you can leave that $600,000 to a trust. As long as the surviving spouse lives, he or she receives the income from that trust. On $600,000 worth of assets, that could be $30,000 or $35,000 per year. At the death of the second spouse, the trust assets go to the trust beneficiaries—probably your children. So you see that you *can* save taxes and *still* provide for your surviving spouse.

Mission: Control

Could the strategy just envisioned have any potential flaws? Unfortunately, yes. For example: Your spouse might squander the money you leave to him or her, beyond the $600,000 that goes into the trust. Or, in the case of his or her second marriage, your spouse might leave this money to his or her children, rather than to yours. Or (also in the case of such a remarriage), your assets might wind up with a spouse's new mate.

These problems can *all* be averted with a QTIP (*qualified terminable interest property*) trust. With these trusts, *all* the income *must* go to the surviving spouse. In case of an emergency, the trustee can use the principal to support the surviving spouse. When the surviving spouse dies, though, the trust assets will go to the trust beneficiaries named by you—probably your own children. Therefore, a QTIP trust provides for your spouse yet lets you control the assets so that they wind up with your children. Plus, the estate tax is deferred through the unlimited marital deduction.

Getting Your Money's Worth

Another type of trust that may be a huge tax saver is a *life-insurance trust*. Often, an estate plan includes a policy covering your life (or your life *and* your spouse's life). At your death, the policy's beneficiaries collect the proceeds, which can be used to pay the estate tax. However, if that policy is owned by you, the proceeds will be *included in* your estate, and half the proceeds will be lost to estate taxes.

Suppose you expect to leave a $2 million estate, so you buy a $700,000 life-insurance policy to cover the expected tax bill. If you die holding the policy, your estate jumps up to $2.7 million, and your tax bill to $1.05 million. You'll have bought a $700,000 policy, but received only $350,000 in benefits.

Because of what we have seen can happen otherwise, life-insurance policies are commonly held in irrevocable trusts. As long as certain rules are followed, and you have no control over the trust that holds the policy, all of the money paid under the policy will be excluded from your taxable estate.

House Rules

If you own a valuable house, you might want to establish a *personal residence trust*, according to the terms of which you give your house to the trust while retaining the right to reside in it for a specified number of years. *After* the trust term, the house can pass to your children, and the delay will greatly reduce the gift tax.

Suppose you're fifty years old and you specify a twenty-year term. You may wind up owing almost a zero gift tax. This would permit you to exclude the house and all future appreciation on it from your taxable estate. You can also use such a trust to transfer a *vacation* house on a discounted basis.

Setting up the trusts mentioned in this chapter might cost a few thousand dollars, plus the ongoing expense of administration and tax preparation. However, this investment will be worthwhile if you wind up saving your family many times that much in estate taxes.

SUMMING UP

• At your death, all of your assets will be valued and the result will be reported to the IRS.

• If your assets total under $600,000, *no* estate tax will be due.

• Any amount *over* $600,000 will be steeply taxed, starting at 37 percent and going as high as 60 percent.

• You can reduce your taxable estate by giving away assets during your lifetime.

• On gifts up to $10,000 per year per recipient ($20,000 from a married couple), *no* gift tax will be due.

• Gifts and bequests between spouses *aren't* taxed, no matter how large.

• Gifts and bequests often are made in trust, to protect assets and to direct them toward certain beneficiaries.

• Married couples can leave up to $1.2 million, free of gift- and estate taxes, by making sure that their children receive up to $600,000 worth of assets at the death of each donor.

• A QTIP trust will permit an older, wealthier spouse to provide for a surviving spouse yet make sure that the estate winds up with designated beneficiaries.

• If you buy life insurance to help pay an estate tax, the policy should be held in an irrevocable trust, outside of your taxable estate.

Part X

At Last, Safety First

36

Protect Your Most Precious Assets

The Health and Well-Being of Yourself and Your Family

On a certain Thanksgiving morning Anne S., a seventy-four-year-old widow weighing a spare 105 pounds, put on her best jewelry as she finished getting ready to go to a friend's home to enjoy a festive Turkey Day celebration. She then drove her new Nissan from the Borough of Queens in New York's metropolitan area to the suburban area of Valley Stream, on Long Island. She was thinking happy thoughts when suddenly two men in a sedan bumped her car from behind, then sideswiped it, and finally drove in front of her, to slow her down.

Because Anne had heard about carjacking, she refused to even stop her car (no less get out of it). Instead, she kept going—over the lawns of private homes when necessary. At one point the men cut her off, and one got out of their car and ran directly at her. "I put the transmission in drive and aimed right at him," she later told the *New York Times*. "I was trying to kill him as the only way of saving my life."

He dodged her, and she threw the car into reverse. The attacker then thrust his arm into her window, which she'd left open—but she kept going in reverse, dragging him almost a block. After that little setback, the outwitted miscreants gave up. And Anne got to have her turkey dinner, *plus* keep the gems and wheels.

If an attempted carjacking can take place on Thanksgiving Day in Nassau County, it can happen anywhere, at any time. In upscale North Dallas, for instance, where Ross Perot and town Mayor Steve Bartlett live, two residents were murdered and twenty others were victims of gunpoint robberies in early 1994 alone. Residents felt forced to switch from Cadillacs to Hondas, to lower their profiles.

Nationwide, a 1991 survey by the National Opinion Research Council found that more than 42 percent of residents in suburbs of major cities are afraid to walk in their own neighborhood at night. Apparently you're never *totally* safe, and neither are your loved ones. Everyone in your family must know what they need to do in order to survive!

Proceed With Caution

In some ways, Anne was lucky. Her assailants had tried to use the old "bump and rob" technique, about which she'd heard. But carjackers have moved on to other tactics. Now, you might be held up—at gunpoint—while you're pumping gas at a self-service station, or perhaps followed home, to have your house looted and your car stolen.

Whenever you're in a car, the threat of carjacking can exist. The American Automobile Association (AAA) has published these tips that you and your family should know about, concerning how to thwart carjackers:

• When you're out in public, look around and get a good view of the entire area.

• If you stop to use a pay phone or buy gas, choose sites that are busy and well-lighted.

• When you're returning home, keep an eye out for pedestrians and other vehicles in the area. Beep your horn so someone in the house knows you've arrived.

• Make sure your driveway and garage area are well-lighted after dark.

• If your car is bumped from behind, don't stop and get out if you have *any* doubts. Drive slowly to the nearest populated service station, police station, hospital, or fire station.

• Always keep your car doors locked, and roll your windows up most of the way. If you're in a doubtful neighborhood, close your windows and use the air-conditioning, if necessary.

The AAA doesn't recommend it, but in some situations you're justified in running a red light or ignoring a stop sign—at that point, getting a ticket is the least of your problems. In addition, everyone in your family should have a first-class *car phone*. Not only can they call 911 for help, if they see someone following them, but also, they won't have to worry about being stranded in case of a flat tire, engine trouble, or such.

Ted L. Gunderson, a security consultant in Santa Monica, California, advises drivers to use well-traveled streets at night. Put any valuables *in the trunk*, rather than exposed inside your car, and never leave any important papers in the glove compartment. In case of a breakdown, place a white handkerchief on the antenna, and sit inside your *locked* car, Gunderson suggests. Also, never accept a lift from a stranger.

In addition to following these precautions, you can buy an *anticarjacking device*. These are becoming increasingly sophisticated. One, for example, comes with a hidden "kill switch." You throw the switch if a carjacker forces you to get out of your car. Three minutes later, after the thief has gone out of shooting range, the car dies. (If you miss the switch you'll miss your car, of course.)

Another device, called Lasso (which sells for $300–$400) begins talking to unauthorized drivers seventy-five seconds after the car is in motion. Thieves and carjackers are told "Get out of my vehicle" because the engine will shut off and loud sirens will turn on. Not only sirens *outside* the vehicle, but also a painful, high-pitched squeal will sound *inside* the car.

Even buying an "armored car" won't help. Well—actually, it might, but it costs at least $40,000 to armor a car (with fiber) and install 2½"-thick window glass so that a 9-mm bullet won't penetrate. If you want "full-metal jacket" protection capable of stopping an armor-piercing projectile, the cost would be around $100,000—plus the price of the car. Following the precautions previously mentioned would seem to be a much more practical approach.

Ultra-Bright

The aforementioned Gunderson, a twenty-seven-year FBI veteran, offers these tips for everyday personal care, which you should pass on to your entire family:

- Use well-traveled, well-lit streets.
- Be alert, and watch for shadows.
- If necessary, use any available object as a weapon, such as an umbrella, shoes, or even your keys.
- Don't be embarrassed to *scream*!
- If you are being followed, cross the street; and if the person also crosses, run to the nearest residence and phone the police.
- Be alert for pickpockets working in pairs, with one jostling you while the other extracts your wallet.
- Carry only small amounts of cash.
- If you carry a handbag, always walk with the clasp facing toward you.
- Never walk alone after dark.
- Avoid shortcuts through dark areas.
- Stay away from doorways, shrubbery, and clumps of trees.
- Never accept rides from strangers.
- Never open your wallet so a stranger can see your identification or how much money you're carrying.
- Never leave a handbag in an unattended location, or carry it open.
- Keep the phone numbers of your local fire and police department handy and, if applicable, the number of your apartment building's security office.

Should you or your family members carry a defensive spray? Mace is made from a chlorine-based tear-gas compound called CN, or chloroacetophenone. However, CN acts by irritating membrane tissues, so it's not always effective against attackers high on drugs or alcohol. Aficionados prefer Mace fortified with pepper.

What about stun guns? They deliver 200,000 volts of electricity (versus 120 volts for a typical home-wiring system), quite enough to stagger most attackers. But then, you have to *touch* your assailant in order for a stun gun to work. Although stun guns are illegal in many areas, if you live in one where they *are* legal, it may be worth paying around $60 to have one you can hold in your hand while you're taking a walk on the wild side.

Raise the Drawbridge!

Your home is supposed to be your castle, a fortress against intruders. But that's no longer automatically the case, so—if you can afford to— move into a secure community. Especially in Nevada and Texas, sub- divisions are being built with gates, walls, and even moats.

Assuming you don't live in such a safe development, you and your family members should know what to do if a burglar is discovered in your house, perhaps at night while the family is asleep. The best strategy, in most cases, is to *get out*, along with the rest of the family. You never know what weapons a burglar might have, and how willing that intruder is to use them. If that's not practical, make noise—turn your radio on full volume, perhaps. If the burglar is actually in your room, play possum. You're really at a disadvantage, so you have to hope that the intruder will only take the money and run. Most bur- glars *won't* attack unless they're frightened.

If you arrive home to see that your house has been broken into, leave it. Get the police before going back in, just in case a burglar is still there. For insurance purposes, take a photo of any damage before cleaning up; then get a copy of the police report.

One way to alert yourself to an intruder is to do this (but first be sure to warn anyone living with you): Whenever you leave home, put (say) a $20 bill just inside the door. If that bait isn't there when you're back home, get out immediately. (You can do the same in a hotel room *if* you're not expecting maid or other service.) When you're at home, don't let door-to-door salespeople in.

Unsafe Deposit

When you leave your house, pick your shopping malls with care— favor those with visible security forces cruising through the parking lot. Even in such malls, park in well-lit areas, however.

For city dwellers especially, one of the most dangerous trips possible is to an automated teller machine (ATM). Marshall N., a New York banker, went to an ATM in mid-Manhattan at 10:30 on a summer night. A man with a knife met him there and "invited" Marshall to make a $200 withdrawal. It was an "offer" that Marshall couldn't refuse.

If you're an ATM user, follow some simple rules. Avoid ATMs in dark, remote places: If you can't get to a safe one at a bank, go to your *supermarket*. Don't go near an ATM if you see someone hanging around, either on foot *or* in a parked car. If you're driving up to an ATM, keep your doors and other windows locked:

Don't register and use a personal identification number (PIN) that someone might guess, such as the last four digits of your phone number. *Never* write down your PIN.

Have your ATM card ready, so you can get in and out of the ATM area as quickly as possible. Put the cash you receive in your pocket or purse right away, so you're not ambling along flashing a wad of bills. Make sure you have your *card* before you leave the ATM, and retain your *receipt*, to prevent anyone from getting your account information. Go with someone you know, if possible—and *don't* hold the door for strangers when entering an enclosed ATM.

Never make a *cash deposit* into an ATM. If there's a foul-up, you won't be able to prove you actually made the deposit!

Ready and Willing

If you're being mugged, should you fight back or give in? Put yourself in the shoes of Brian H., a Canadian businessman who had just finished dinner with a countryman in London. As they left the restaurant and headed back toward their hotel, they encountered five skinheads who were making martial-arts moves.

One of the skinheads asked them for money. According to the conventional wisdom, Brian should have handed over his wallet and been happy to escape without injury. However, in the hair-trigger 1990s, meekness may invite aggression. Frustrated criminals may injure you, even kill you, if you're too passive.

Brian, who had some martial-arts training himself, set himself for action, sending a subtle signal to the skinheads that he wouldn't be an easy mark. At the same time, he kept on walking and making conversation with the skinheads. "I've spent all my money," he told them. The skinheads wound up giving Brian a 50-pence coin!

If you're ever involved in anything even resembling *this* confrontation, you *also* may not be of a mind to give in docilely. If so, keep up a conversation with your would-be muggers. Tell them you're just an average working man (or woman), just as they are. While you're talking, though, look for a chance to get away or yell for help. If you *truly* know what you're doing, perhaps launch a preemptive strike. (If none of the above applies, you can try either running, or giving in.)

The best defense is offense: Avoid confrontations by staying alert. For example, never stop to look at your watch if someone asks you for the time. Make a guess, and keep walking.

What should you do if someone comes up behind you and puts an arm around your throat? Spin around and face the bugger. Now your opponent *can't* choke you because it's the muscles at the *back* of your neck that are being squeezed. Even if you have never had any martial-arts training whatsoever, you can still strike at his groin, kneecap, face, or throat, with whatever it takes to do that. (*Hint:* A man's groin is *extremely* sensitive, so give it your best shot. He more than likely will release you—and not be able to catch you when you flee. *Also:* you'll have two free arms, to his one or none.)

You may want to make sure that everyone in your family knows basic self-defense techniques. Many martial-arts instructors have special programs for people who *don't* care to earn a black belt but *do* want to know how to defend themselves.

Buddy System

If you come from a wealthy family, or even if you're only moderately wealthy, you're a potential kidnap victim. Hire a driver, if you can afford it. Not only will that give you less stress and more work time, but also it will provide a defender in case of a kidnap attempt. You might want to apply for a sidearm (gun) permit, too. Just make sure you take enough training so you know how to use it if you're threatened.

Vary your routine. *Don't* eat the same meal in the same restaurant every day; *don't* regularly jog the same route at the same time. Dress conservatively, and save any jewelry for private occasions.

Skip vanity license plates, because they draw attention to yourself. If you think you're being followed while in your car, *don't* drive home. Go somewhere public and official—such as a police station or hospital.

Kid Stuff

Of course, children, too, can be kidnap victims—but there are *some* devices that might well help protect your kids. The Child Guardian ($50 from Direkt Inc.) allows a parent to beep a child. And, if the child feels threatened, he or she can sound a loud alarm.

For around $30, you can buy a Personal Attack Alarm, sold by

Quorum International. These are hand-held devices that enable you to pull a pin and activate a 100-decibel alarm, roughly equal to the noise a commercial jet makes on takeoff and many New York subway trains create. (These so-called "panic buttons" also may be appropriate for adults who go out alone or stay home alone.)

Whether or not you go in for high-tech protection, make sure your kids know the basics: *Don't* talk with strangers, and *don't* go off with anyone. If an adult tries to abduct your child, that young one shouldn't just cry, since tears can make a confrontation seem like a normal parent–child altercation. Instead, your child should keep saying "I don't know you," over and over, *as loud as possible*. If anything will attract help from passersby, *that* will do it.

Also, don't buy any clothes for a child with his or her name on display, and don't sew on name tags where they're visible. Those clues make it all too easy for a stranger to call the child by name and say "Your Mom sent me to get you"—or some other come-on line.

For information on Child Lures Community Plan, a Vermont-based program that teaches children how to resist enticements from would-be abductors, call 802-985-8458.

Learn Your Lesson

Don't send your child off to college without checking on the crime climate there! The federal Crime Awareness and Campus Security Act (which took effect in late 1992), requires most colleges to annually publish crime statistics for the past three years, including on-campus and near-campus murders, rapes, robberies, assaults, and arrests for weapons possession.

In addition, colleges *must* describe their campus security programs. On a campus visit, when you check out the dorms and the academic facilities, stop by the admissions office and get a copy of the school's crime-prevention pamphlet. Also, go to its security office and talk with the officers there, to get a personal impression of the magnitude of the crime problem, and the effectiveness of the security department.

Shop Before You Drop

Many of the personal-security devices mentioned in this chapter, and elsewhere in this book, are available from Safety Zone (call 800-999-3030 for a catalog). Here's a sampling of the 1994 offerings:

• Water-resistant Electro Flares for use in case of highway emergencies (two for $15.95)

• A keychain alarm that emits a shrill noise meant to scare off attackers, and converts to a door-, window-, or fire alarm ($15.95)

• Peppergard, Mace, and Spray Stunner ($14.95–$22.95)

• Bubble Box Safe for travel ($39.95)

• "Leg Safe" and "Waist Safe" ($9.95) to hold valuables while traveling

• Door Jammer ($17.95), a steel brace that keeps intruders out of your home or hotel room

• Safe-T-Man ($119.95), a life-size simulated male meant to indicate you're not alone, whether at home or in your car

For free pamphlets such as "How to Be Streetwise and Safe," "Got a Minute? You Could Stop Crime," "How to Crimeproof Your Business," "How to Protect Your Home," and "How to Protect Your Children," write to the Superintendent of Documents, U.S. Government Printing Office, Washington, DC 20402.

SUMMING UP

• Today, *defensive* driving means keeping an eye out for carjackers, and using *offensive* measures to thwart them, if necessary.

• Wherever you go, stay in well-populated, well-lighted areas whenever possible.

• Instead of letting your guard down when you're home, make it a point *not* to open the door to strangers.

• Automated teller machines lure cash-hungry thieves, so be wary of people hanging around when you use an ATM.

• If you are approached by potential muggers, engage them in conversation *while* you seek a chance to escape.

• Teach your kids to keep away from strangers, and *don't* dress them in anything that reveals their name.

• Before you send a child to college, find out how many violent *crimes* have been committed there, and how serious the school is about physical *security*.

Index

255